は じ め に

　英語が苦手で、生涯、英語を勉強するつもりのなかったわたしが、NHKの海外向け番組「Your Japanese Kitchen」に出演することになって、できないながらも英語で自分の料理を伝えることになりました。2007年4月のことでした。そのときから、自分のレシピを英語で書けること、英語で話せるようになることを目標にしてコツコツと勉強を続けてきました。

　2014年からハワイ州立大学付属のカピオラニ・コミュニティー・カレッジで年に2回、料理を教えています。日本料理は「工程が多くて大変そう」とか、「時間がかかる」という印象を少しでも変えられるように楽しんで料理することを伝えています。
自分自身の経験を振り返ると、英語と料理はとても似ていると思います。わたしは、自分がいちばん言いたいフレーズを覚えて、それを使うことから始めました。料理も同じように、まずは一品、自分の好きなものをつくれるようになると、料理が楽しくなります。家族や友人のためにつくったり、海外の人をもてなしたり、料理を通じて人の輪はどんどん広がります。

　本書には「Your Japanese Kitchen」で外国の方に向けて発信してきたレシピや、ハワイで教えて喜ばれた料理をはじめ、自分のレシピの中でも特に外国の人に覚えてほしい料理を厳選して紹介しています。初めて和食に触れる人にもわかりやすいように基本を押さえ、海外でもつくりやすいように材料なども工夫しました。

　日本の方にとってもこのレシピはきっと楽しんでもらえると思います。料理のほかにも和食で使う道具や、わたしが日々の暮らしで大切にしていることなども紹介しています。この本を通じて日本の家庭料理を多くの方々につくっていただけたらとてもうれしいです。

2018年5月　栗原はるみ

Foreword

I had never been good at English, and I did not imagine I would ever study English during my lifetime. However, as it happened, in April 2007 I appeared on "Your Japanese Kitchen", an NHK program broadcast overseas, where I began to introduce Japanese home cooking with my poor English. Since then, I have continued to study English with the goal of being able to write my own recipe and convey myself in English.

I started teaching cooking twice a year at Kapi'olani Community College of the University of Hawaii from 2014. People often say, "Japanese cooking is difficult and has so many procedures", or "Japanese cooking is very time-consuming". I want to change that image and convey that it is fun to cook.

Looking back on my experiences, I have found that English and cooking are, in a sense, very similar. With English, I used to memorize the phrases I like to use the most and began by using them. The same thing can be applied to cooking. Begin by making what you particularly like. You will then gradually become interested in cooking. You will cook for your family and friends or entertain your guests from overseas with your homemade dishes. This way, you can enhance your bonds with other people through cooking.

The recipes in this book include recipes I have introduced to people outside Japan through the program "Your Japanese Kitchen", and the recipes that were popular when I taught in Hawaii. I carefully handpicked the recipes that I especially want people overseas to learn. I have tried to explain Japanese dishes simply, beginning with the basic steps, so that people who have never tried Japanese food will nevertheless be able to understand. I have also tried to choose ingredients that are available overseas.

I'm sure that Japanese people will also find these recipes delightful.In addition to Japanese dishes, I have introduced Japanese cooking utensils, and have shared my thoughts on things I cherish in my daily life. I would be happy if this book could give more people an opportunity to try Japanese home cooking.

Harumi Kurihara, May 2018

序章 | PREFACE |

1

CHAPTER 1

MEAT & FISH　肉と魚のおかず

2

CHAPTER 2

VEGETABLES　野菜のおかず

3

CHAPTER 3

RICE, NOODLES & MORE　ご飯もの、麺、その他

CHAPTER 4
DESSERTS　甘味

白いエプロン
White apron

白いエプロンはわたしの大切な仕事着です。白は汚れやすいという理由で敬遠されがちですが、汚れが目立つからいいのです。色の濃いものは汚れに気づきにくいものです。汚れたらきれいに洗濯してアイロンをかける。そうすると、また大切に使おうという気持ちになります。

刺しゅうで名前も入れています。エプロンをつけるたびに自分の名前を見ると仕事に責任を持たなければいけないと思うと同時に、きょうも一日楽しく過ごそうと思えるのです。

A white apron is my important work clothes. People tend to avoid wearing white because it can be a challenge to keep it looking white and stain-free. But this is precisely why it is better. It is harder to notice the stain with a darker colored apron. But with the white one, you will wash and iron it promptly if it stains, and this will motivate you to use it with extra care.

The apron is also embroidered with my name. Therefore, every time I put on the apron, I see my name, and it reminds me that I need to be responsible for my own work. And at the same time, it makes me look forward to another joyful day.

KURIHARA

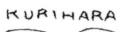

この本の使い方

● この本で使用している計量カップは200ml、
  計量スプーンは大さじ1＝15ml、小さじ1＝5ml です。
  1cc＝1ml です。すりきりで量ります。

● でき上がりの分量（4人分）や（2人分）はあくまで目安です。

● だしは、22ページのように昆布とかつお節でとったものです。

● しょうゆは濃口しょうゆ、砂糖は上白糖、小麦粉は薄力粉のことです。

● 電子レンジの時間は出力600Wの機種を目安にしています（＊）。

● 温度単位には摂氏（℃＝Centigrade）と華氏（°F＝Fahrenheit）があります。
  この本では日本で採用されている摂氏（℃）で表記しています。
  ちなみに摂氏と華氏の換算は以下のとおりです。
  ℃＝（°F－32）×5／9　　　°F＝9／5℃＋32

● 重量は g で表記しています。
  1g（gram）＝0.035 oz（ounces）　1oz（ounce）＝28.35g（grams）

● 長さは mm、cm で表記しています。
  1cm＝0.39inches　1inch＝2.54cm

● 材料表の大さじは、tablespoon を略して tbsp、
  小さじは、teaspoon を略して tsp と表記します。
  例）　しょうゆ　大さじ2　　2 tbsp soy sauce
  　　　砂糖　小さじ1　　　　1 tsp sugar

＊ 700Wの場合は約0.8倍、500Wの場合は約1.2倍にしてください。
＊ 電子レンジは、金属および金属製の部分がある容器や非耐熱ガラスの容器、
  漆器、木・竹・紙製品、耐熱温度が140℃未満の樹脂製容器などを使うと
  故障や事故の原因となることがありますのでご注意ください。
＊ 調理器具は、各メーカーの使用説明書などをよくお読みのうえ、
  正しくお使いください。

How to use this book

- Cup measurements in this book are 200ml. 1 tablespoon is 15ml, and a teaspoon is 5ml. 1cc is the same as 1ml. Level measures are used.
- Quantities described as "Serves 4" or "Serves 2" should be treated as estimations.
- As described on page 23, dashi is extracted from kelp and dried bonito.
- In this book, soy sauce refers to regular soy sauce (koikuchi); the sugar used is white sugar; flour refers to plain flour.
- Microwave oven times are estimated using a 600W model as reference.
- Fahrenheit (°F) and Centigrade (°C) are both units of temperature measurement, but in this book only the standard Japanese measurement of Centigrade is listed. Conversion from Centigrade to Fahrenheit is as follows:

  $$°C = (°F - 32) \times 5 / 9 \quad °F = 9 / 5 °C + 32$$
- Weight measurements are given in grams.

  1g (gram) = 0.035oz (ounces)

  1oz (ounce) = 28.35g (grams)
- Length measurements are given in mm and cm.

  1cm = 0.39inches   1inch = 2.54cm
- Materials are abbreviated as follows:

  tablespoon = tbsp, teaspoon = tsp.

  Example: "2 tablespoons soy sauce" is indicated as "2 tbsp soy sauce" and "1 teaspoon sugar" is written as "1 tsp sugar."

おいしいご飯を炊きましょう

Let's cook some delicious rice

わたしはご飯が大好きなので、いつもおいしく食べるためにいろいろな工夫をしています。日本ではご飯は炊飯器で炊くのが主流になっていますが、お鍋でも簡単に炊けます。お米の研ぎ方、ご飯の炊き方にはいろいろな方法がありますが、ここでご紹介するのはわたしのやり方です。皆さんも自分好みの炊き方を見つけて、水加減などを調節しながら試してみてくださいね。

I like Japanese-style cooked rice, which is why I have been making all kinds of efforts to cook delicious rice. Japanese people usually use a rice cooker to cook their rice. Even without this convenient tool, however, you can easily cook rice in a pan or a pot.

There are various ways of preparing rice, but I will introduce my own style in this book. I hope you will find your own favorite style by trying several different methods, adjusting the amount of water used, and so on.

ご 飯 の 炊 き 方

1. ボウルに米カップ2を入れて水を注ぎ、静かにかき混ぜ、濁った水を捨てる。
2. 手のひらのつけ根で米粒どうしをこすり合わせるようにして研ぎ、流水ですすいで水けをきる。これを水が透明になるまで繰り返す。
3. ざるに上げ、15分ほどおく。
4. 鍋に米を入れ、同量の水を注ぐ。柔らかめに炊きたい場合は水を少し多めに、堅めに炊きたい場合は水をやや少なめにする。
5. ふたをし、火にかける。沸騰したら弱火にし、10～12分ほど炊く。
6. 火を止めて10分ほど蒸らしてからふたを取り、かき混ぜる。

How to prepare rice

1. Put 2 cups of rice in a bowl. Fill with cold water and stir the rice gently with your hand. Discard the cloudy water.
2. Rub the grains gently against each other with the heel of your hand. Rinse under cold running water and drain. Continue rubbing and rinsing until the water becomes clear.
3. Drain the rice in a strainer. Let it stand for 15 minutes.
4. Put the rice in a pan. Add the same amount of water to the pan as rice. For a softer texture, add a little more water; for more texture, use a little less water.
5. Cover the pan and turn the heat on high. Bring to a boil and simmer for 10-12 minutes over low heat.
6. Turn off the heat and let stand for 10 minutes. Remove the lid and stir the rice.

ご飯が炊けたら
おにぎりに

The rice is cooked
-now let's make "Onigiri"
(rice balls)

炊きたてのご飯で握るおにぎりは格
別のおいしさです。中に入れる具で
いちばん好きなのは糸昆布のつくだ
煮。それ以外にも梅干し、焼いたさ
け、たらこ、ちりめんざんしょうなど
いろいろあります。自由に好みの具
を入れてつくってみてください。

Rice balls made of freshly steamed
rice taste especially good. My
favorite filling is julienned kelp
tsukudani (boiled down in sweetened soy sauce). There are many
different types of fillings to choose
from: *umeboshi* (pickled Japanese
plum), grilled salmon, cod roe,
dried young sardines seasons with
sansho pepper, and so on. Please
feel free to make rice balls with
fillings of your taste.

おにぎり

ご飯　適宜　　　　　　　　［具］
のり　適宜　　　　　　　　梅干し　適宜
塩　　　　　　　　　　　　昆布のつくだ煮　適宜
　　　　　　　　　　　　　塩ざけ（焼いてほぐしたもの）　適宜

1. ラップにご飯をのせて
中央に小さな穴をあけ
る。大さじ1程度の好
みの具をのせ、その上
にご飯をのせて軽く
握り、ラップを外す。

2. 手を水につけ、塩少々
を手のひらにまぶす。
ご飯をのせて丸く握る。

3. のりを巻く。

"Onigiri" (rice balls)

cooked rice
nori seaweed
salt

[fillings]

umeboshi (Japanese pickled plum)

kombu *tsukudani*
    (kombu kelp simmered in salty-sweet sauce)

salted salmon (grilled and flaked)

1. Place some rice onto a plastic wrap. Make a small dent in the middle, and put the filling of your choice (about 1 tbsp) there. Place more rice on top and shape into a ball. Remove the plastic wrap.

2. Soak your hands in water. Sprinkle a little salt on your palm. Then put the rice on it and shape into a ball.

3. Wrap the rice balls with nori seaweed.

きちんとだしをとりましょう

Prepare dashi in the proper way

昆布とかつお節でとるこのだしは、日本料理の
いちばん基本となるだしです。今は海外でも粉
末だしやティーバッグのだしなどが手に入るよう
になり、和食が浸透して拡がってうれしいかぎ
りですが、まずはきちんととっただしのおいし
さを知ってほしいと思います。火加減とタイミ
ングさえ気をつければ、だれでもおいしいだし
が、思っていたより簡単にとることができます。

Dashi (introduced in this book) is a Japanese
soup stock made from kelp and dried bonito
flakes, and is a base of Japanese cuisine. Re-
cently, dashi stocks which come in powder
and tea bags have become available overseas,
which has helped to spread the popularity of
washoku. Although I welcome this situation,
I wish first, that you taste the deliciousness
of authentic dashi made in the proper way.
As long as you exercise care with the heating
and timing, anyone can make a tasty dashi –
it's easier than you might expect.

だ し の と り 方

水　カップ6（1200ml）
昆布（10cm角）　1枚
かつお節　40g

1. 昆布は軽く洗って紙タオルでよくふき、分量の水に約30分つける。

2. 火にかけ、沸騰する直前に昆布を取り除き、煮立てる。かつお節を加えて少し煮て、もう一度沸騰したら火を止める。

3. かつお節が鍋底に沈むまでそのままおき、ざるでこす。

How to make dashi (soup stock)

6 cups (1200ml) water
10cm-square kombu kelp
40g dried bonito flakes

1. Rinse the kombu lightly, and wipe thoroughly with a paper towel. Soak it in the water for about 30 minutes.
2. Turn the heat on high. Remove the kombu just before the water comes to a boil. Bring the water to a boil, and add the bonito flakes. When it comes to a boil, turn the heat off.
3. Let stand until the flakes sink to the bottom of the pot. Then strain through a sieve.

だしでみそ汁

Miso soup with dashi

上手にだしがとれたら、まずはみそ汁をつくってみましょう。
みそ汁はわたしも大好きで、毎日欠かさず飲んでいます。具は、残った野菜でつくったり、冷蔵庫を整理・チェックしていろいろな組み合わせを考えながらつくっています。今回は日本の家庭でいちばんつくられている豆腐とわかめのみそ汁をご紹介します。

If a good dashi is ready, first start with miso soup.
I like miso soup so much that I eat it each and every day. As ingredients, I often use leftover vegetables from my refrigerator. I check what's in the refrigerator and then clean it out by taking various combinations of ingredients for use in a miso soup.
In this book, I introduce the most commonly made miso soup in Japanese homes, one with tofu and wakame.

豆腐とわかめのみそ汁

【 材料4人分 】

絹ごし豆腐　1丁
わかめ（塩蔵）　30g
だし　カップ4（800ml）
みそ　大さじ4

1. 豆腐は1cm角に切る。わかめは水につけて塩抜きし、食べやすく切る。わかめはあらかじめ器に入れておく。
2. 鍋にだしを沸かし、豆腐を加え、みそを溶き入れる。
3. わかめの入った器に熱いみそ汁を注ぐ。

Miso soup with tofu and wakame

[Serves 4]

---

1 pack soft tofu

30g wakame seaweed (salt-preserved)

4 cups (800ml) dashi

4 tbsp miso

1. Cut the tofu into 1cm cubes. Soak the wakame in water to take the salt out, and cut it into bite-sized pieces. Place the wakame into a soup bowl.

2. Bring the dashi to a boil. Add the tofu. Add the miso and dissolve.

3. Pour the hot miso soup over the bowl of wakame.

箸置き
Hashioki (chopstick rest)

箸をテーブルに置くときに使うものですが、大きさの違うものをいろ
いろ持っていると便利です。わたしは少し大きめのものにレモンや
漬物などちょっと添えたいものをのせたり、小さいグラスのコース
ターにしたりと、いろいろな使い方を楽しんでいます。

This tableware is used to place chopsticks on the table. It is handy
to have sets of various sizes. I enjoy using them in many different
ways. I put garnishes, such as lemon slices or pickles on the larger
sized ones. Sometimes I use them as coasters for small glasses.

1

· MEAT & FISH

肉と魚のおかず

豚のしょうが焼き

Ginger pork

簡単な料理ですが、何度もつくり続けて、よりおいしくなればと工夫を重ねてきたレシピです。肉を焼く前に常温に戻しておくことと、たれをからめたらあまりおかずにすぐに焼くことが大きなポイントです。

This is a simple and easy dish, but I have repeatedly made this dish trying various methods so that I can find an even better taste. The important point is that you take the meat out of the fridge beforehand to have it at room temperature when it is cooked. Also, once you dress the meat with sauce, immediately start grilling it in a pan.

豚のしょうが焼き

豚肩ロース薄切り肉　300g
おろししょうが　大さじ1
しょうゆ　大さじ4
みりん　大さじ3
サラダ油　適宜
ポテトサラダ（104ページ参照）

1. しょうゆ、みりん、おろししょうがを混ぜ合わせ、豚肉を2〜3分つける。
2. フライパンを強火にかけてサラダ油を熱し、豚肉を焼き色がつくまで両面を手早く焼く。
   * 何回か焼く場合は、フライパンを洗ってから使う。
3. 皿にポテトサラダと豚肉を盛り、豚肉の焼き汁をかける。

* 豚の薄切り肉が手に入らない場合は、ブロック肉を半冷凍してからできるだけ薄く切る。ラップではさみ、麺棒でたたいて薄くのばす。

Ginger pork

300g sliced pork
  shoulder loin

1 tbsp grated ginger

4 tbsp soy sauce

3 tbsp mirin

vegetable oil

potato salad
  (see page 104)

1. Combine the soy sauce, mirin, and grated ginger. Marinate the pork in the mixture for a few minutes.

2. Heat some vegetable oil in a frying pan over high heat, and briskly sear both sides of the pork slices until brown.

   * If you need to repeat this process several times, make sure to wash the frying pan.

3. Put some potato salad and the ginger pork onto a serving plate. Pour the pan juice from step 2 on the pork.

   * If you can't get sliced pork, half-freeze the pork loin and then slice it as thinly as possible. Place each slice between plastic wrap and tap with a rolling pin to make it thinner.

肉じゃが

"Nikujaga"
(beef and potato stew)

何度も何度もつくっているけれど、いまだに「あぁ、こういうことが大切だったのか」と気づく料理があります。肉じゃがもそのひとつ。簡単そうに見えて、おいしくつくるのは意外にむずかしいのです。
いちばん大切なのは、じゃがいもの表面が透き通るまでよく炒めること。そうすると味の含みがぐんとよくなります。

I have some dishes I cook often and yet every time I cook them, I will make a new discovery and I will say, "I have never noticed this important thing before." This is one such dish. It may look easy to cook, but in fact it is difficult to cook it in such a way that it satisfies your taste buds.
The most important thing is to stir-fry the potatoes until their surface becomes translucent. This makes it easier for the potatoes to absorb the flavor of the stock and seasonings.

肉じゃが

牛薄切り肉　250g

じゃがいも　4〜5コ（600g）

玉ねぎ　2コ

だし　カップ1+1/2（300ml）

しょうゆ　大さじ5〜6

みりん　大さじ3

砂糖　大さじ4〜4+1/2

酒　大さじ1

サラダ油　大さじ1

1. じゃがいもは皮をむいて4等分に切る。5〜6分ほど水にさらし、水けをよくふく。玉ねぎは4〜6等分のくし形切りにする。牛肉は一口大に切る。

2. フライパンを中火にかけ、サラダ油を熱する。じゃがいもを入れ、表面が透き通るまでしっかり炒める。玉ねぎを加え、さらに炒める。

3. だし、しょうゆ、みりん、砂糖、酒を加えて煮る。アクを取り、落としぶたをし、じゃがいもが柔らかくなるまで10〜12分煮る。牛肉を広げながら入れ、肉に火が通ったらよく混ぜて火を止め、そのままおいてなじませる。

"Nikujaga" (beef and potato stew)

[Serves 4]

250g thinly sliced beef
600g/4-5 potatoes
2 onions
1+1/2 cups(300ml) dashi
5-6 tbsp soy sauce
3 tbsp mirin
4-4+1/2 tbsp sugar
1 tbsp sake
1 tbsp vegetable oil

1. Peel the potatoes and cut each into four pieces. Soak in water for 5-6 minutes and wipe well. Cut the onions into 4-6 wedges. Cut the beef into bite-sized pieces.

2. Heat the oil on medium in a frying pan. Add the potatoes and stir-fry until their surface are translucent. Add the onions and continue to stir-fry.

3. Add the dashi, soy sauce, mirin, sugar, and sake, and simmer. Skim the surface and put a drop-lid on. Simmer for 10-12 minutes until the potatoes are soft. Then add the beef, while spreading each slices, and cook through. Mix well, and turn off the heat and let stand.

なすと牛肉のみそ煮

Eggplant and beef
simmered in miso

煮ても、焼いても、揚げてもと、なすほど
使い勝手のいい野菜もありません。
好きな食べ方はいろいろありますが、こっ
てりと煮たこのなすもそのひとつ。コクの
あるみそ味で白いご飯によく合います。な
すは少し大きめに切ると、揚げたなすのと
ろりとした食感がより楽しめます。

Eggplant is the most convenient vegetable because it can be delicious when
cooked in any style, including simmered, grilled, or deep-fried.
I like many eggplant dishes, and this
simmered eggplant in savory sauce is
one of them. The rich miso taste goes
very well with white rice. By cutting the
eggplant into larger bite-sized pieces,
you can enjoy the texture of the deep-
fried eggplant that melts in your mouth.

なすと牛肉のみそ煮

【 材料 4人分 】

なす　7〜9コ（700g）
牛切り落とし肉　200g

［煮汁］
だし　カップ1（200ml）
しょうゆ　大さじ3
みりん　大さじ3
砂糖　大さじ3
みそ　大さじ2〜3
豆板醤（トーバンジャン）
　　小さじ2

揚げ油　適宜
サラダ油　大さじ1
おろししょうが　適宜

1. 煮汁のだしと調味料を合わせておく。
2. 牛肉は、大きければ食べやすい大きさに切る。
3. なすはヘタを落として半分に切り、水にさらしてアクを抜き、水けをよくふく。鍋に揚げ油を熱し、なすを素揚げにして中まで火を通す。
4. 熱したフライパンにサラダ油を入れ、牛肉を炒める。
5. 肉に火が通ったら煮汁を加え、再び煮立ったらなすを加える。途中アクが出たら取り除き、5〜10分煮て火を止め、味をなじませる。
6. 汁ごと器に盛り、好みでおろししょうがを添える。

Eggplant and beef simmered in miso

[Serves 4]

7-9 eggplants(700g)
200g beef trimmings

[sauce]
1 cup(200ml)dashi
3 tbsp soy sauce
3 tbsp mirin
3 tbsp sugar
2-3 tbsp miso
2 tsp *To-Ban-Jan*

vegetable oil
  for deep-frying
1 tbsp vegetable oil
grated ginger
  --- for garnish

1. Combine the dashi and other ingredients for sauce.
2. Cut the beef into bite-sized pieces, if needed.
3. Cut the stem off the eggplants, cut in half lengthwise, and soak in water to remove the bitterness. Then drain well and pat dry. Heat the deep-frying oil in the frying pan, and deep-fry the eggplants until they are cooked through.
4. Heat the oil in a frying pan and sauté the beef.
5. When the beef is cooked, add the sauce. When it comes to a boil, add the eggplants. Skim the surface and simmer for 5 to 10 minutes. Turn off the heat and let stand.
6. Place in a serving bowl with the sauce. Garnish with some grated ginger to taste.

サーロインステーキ
のみそづけ

Sirloin steak marinated in miso

食材をみそづけにする調理法は、日本料理
では古くから伝えられています。味つけだ
けでなく、保存もきくので便利です。肉以
外にも、魚や野菜でもつくることができます。
肉は焦げやすいので、焼くときは2cm幅く
らいに切ってから焼くと、厚い部分も端の
薄い部分もそれぞれちょうどいい焼き加減
に調節することができます。お好みでわさ
びや七味を添えても。

Marinating ingredients with miso, which
is called *misozuke* in Japan, is a traditional
way of cooking that we have had in Japan
since long ago. It is useful as it not only
gives richness to the taste but also keeps
the food longer. You can also use fish or
vegetables instead of meat.
To avoid the meat getting burnt, cut it into
2cm-wide slices. This way, you can remove each piece from the heat just in time
when it is well cooked.If you like, serve
with grated wasabi or *shichimi* (seven-
flavor chili pepper).

サーロインステーキのみそづけ

サーロインステーキ
　（2cm厚さ）　4枚
わさび・すだち　各適宜

［みそだれ］
みそ　400g
酒　カップ1/2（100ml）
みりん　カップ1（200ml）
砂糖　60〜80g

1. みそだれをつくる。鍋にみそ、酒、み
   りん、砂糖を合わせ、弱火で絶えず
   かき混ぜながら、とろみがつくまで
   焦がさないように約20分煮詰める。
   * このみそだれは、冷蔵庫で3週間ほ
     ど保存可能。
2. ステーキの両面にみそだれを片面に
   つき大さじ2ずつぬる。ラップをし、
   冷蔵庫で1〜2日おく。
   * そのまま冷凍保存もできる。
3. みそだれをへらなどで取り除き、食
   べやすい大きさに切り分ける。
4. 両面を焼き網で焼く。器に盛り、好
   みの野菜の炒め物、わさび、すだち
   を添える。

Sirloin steak marinated in miso

[Serves 4]

---

4 sirloin steaks
(2cm thick)
wasabi and sudachi
--- to serve

[miso marinade]
400g miso
1/2 cup(100ml) sake
1 cup(200ml) mirin
60-80g sugar

1. Make the miso marinade: Combine the miso, sake, mirin, and sugar in a pan and bring to a boil. Keep stirring over low heat to avoid burning, and boil down for about 20 minutes until the sauce thickens.
   * This marinade can keep for up to 3 weeks in the refrigerator.
2. Spread 2 tablespoons of the marinade on each side of the steaks and cover with plastic wrap. Let them stand in the refrigerator for 1-2 days.
   * They can be kept in the freezer as they are.
3. Remove the marinade from the steaks with a spatula and cut into bite-sized pieces.
4. Grill the steaks on both sides. Serve with stir-fried vegetables, wasabi, and sudachi.

筑 前 煮

Simmered vegetables with chicken,
Chikuzen-style

お正月料理によく登場する料理ですが、わたしは、一年を通して
よくつくっています。材料を一緒に煮るので、火の通りが均一にな
るよう、大きさをそろえて切ることと、入れる順序が大切です。
乱切り、いちょう切り、半月切りなど、日本ならではの切り方をご
紹介したくて、ここではあえて野菜の切り方を変えてつくりました。

This is one of the popular dishes served at New Year's. In my
home, however, I cook this throughout the year. The important
point in cooking this dish is to cut the ingredients into evenly-
sized pieces or slices, and to put them into a pan in the correct
order so that they cook evenly.
Because I wanted to introduce to you various Japanese ways of
cutting vegetables, I used several techniques.

筑 前 煮

鶏もも肉（骨なし）　250g

ごぼう　1本（180g）

にんじん　1本（200g）

ゆでたけのこ　小1本（150g）

れんこん　1本（200g）

こんにゃく　1枚（200g）

干ししいたけ　4枚

サラダ油　大さじ1～2

だし　カップ1+1/2（300ml）

しょうゆ　大さじ4

砂糖　大さじ4

みりん　大さじ2

酒　大さじ2

1. 干ししいたけはできるだけ少ない水につけて時間をかけて戻す。水けを軽く絞って軸を取り、4等分に切る。

2. 鶏肉は一口大に切る。

3. ごぼうは皮をむいて2cm幅の斜め切りにし、水にさらして水けをよくきる。

4. にんじんは皮をむき、2cm厚さの半月切りにする。たけのこは乱切りにする。

5. れんこんは皮をむいて2cm幅のいちょう切りにする。水にさらし、水けをよくきる。

6. こんにゃくは熱湯でサッとゆで、ざるに上げて水けをよくきる。粗熱が取れたら一口大に手でちぎる。

7. 深めのフライパンを熱し、サラダ油を入れ、鶏肉を炒める。ごぼう、にんじん、こんにゃく、しいたけ、たけのこ、れんこんの順に炒める。足りなければ少し油を足す。

8. だし、しょうゆ、砂糖、みりん、酒を加え、煮立ったらアクを取り、落としぶたをして煮汁が少なくなるまで約15分煮含める。

Simmered vegetables with chicken, *Chikuzen*-style

[Serves 4]

250g boneless chicken thighs

1 burdock (180g)

1 carrot (200g)

1 small bamboo shoot (150g), boiled

1 lotus root (200g)

1 block of konnyaku (200g)

4 dried shiitake mushrooms

1-2 tbsp vegetable oil

1+1/2 cups (300ml) dashi

4 tbsp soy sauce

4 tbsp sugar

2 tbsp mirin

2 tbsp sake

1. Soak the dried shiitake mushrooms in just enough water to cover, take the time to let it soften. Squeeze lightly and cut the stems off, then cut into 4 pieces.

2. Cut the chicken into bite-sized pieces.

3. Peel the burdock and cut diagonally into 2cm-thick pieces. Soak in water and drain well.

4. Peel the carrot and cut into 2cm-thick half-moons(*hangetsu-giri*). (see page 280) Cut the bamboo shoot into *ran-giri* pieces. (see page 281)

5. Peel the lotus root and cut into 2cm-thick quarter-rounds(*icho-giri*). (see page 280) Soak in water and drain well.

6. Blanch the konnyaku and drain well. Tear into bite-sized pieces when cool.

7. Heat the oil in a deep frying pan and stir-fry the chicken. Add the burdock, carrot, konnyaku, shiitake mushrooms, bamboo shoot and lotus root and stir-fry in this order. Add a little more oil if necessary.

8. Add the dashi, soy sauce, sugar, mirin, sake. When it comes to a boil, skim the surface and put a drop-lid on. Simmer for about 15 minutes or until the sauce is reduced.

マカロニグラタン

Macaroni gratin

マカロニ、えび、玉ねぎ、マッシュルーム、鶏肉が入ったこのグラタンは、どの家庭でもつくられている日本の洋食。日本人が考えた最高傑作ともいえると思います。
チーズは、あふれるくらいたっぷりとのせるとおいしそうな焼き上がりに。ご飯にもよく合うので、わたしはしょうゆをちょっとたらして一緒に食べるのが好きです。

This is a common Western-style dish that many Japanese families prepare at home. This gratin contains macaroni, shrimp, onion, mushrooms, and chicken. I have to say this Japanese-style gratin is one of the best dishes the Japanese have created. Topping it with plenty of cheese will make this more delicious. It also goes well with steamed white rice. I usually put a little soy sauce on this gratin so it goes even better with white rice.

マカロニグラタン

【 材料 4人分 】

えび　250g

鶏もも肉　1枚

玉ねぎ　1/2コ

マッシュルーム缶　1缶（100g）

マカロニ　100g

ピザ用チーズ　150g

[ホワイトソース]

バター　40g

小麦粉　50g

牛乳　カップ2+1/2（500ml）

生クリーム　カップ1（200ml）

塩　小さじ1/2〜1

こしょう　少々

サラダ油・塩・こしょう
　　各適宜

[下準備] オーブンを230℃に温めておく。

1. 玉ねぎは薄切りにする。

2. えびは殻をむき、背ワタを取る。きれいに洗い、水けをよくふく。

3. 鶏肉は一口大に切る。

4. マッシュルームは缶から出して汁けをきる。

5. ホワイトソースをつくる。フライパンにバターを溶かし、小麦粉をふり入れて弱火で2〜3分、焦がさないように炒める。牛乳を少しずつ加えてとろみがつくまでよく混ぜながら5分ほど煮る。生クリームを加え、少し煮て、塩、こしょうで味を調える。

6. マカロニは袋の表示を参考にゆでる。ゆで上がったらざるに上げる。

7. フライパンにサラダ油少々を熱し、えびを炒め、軽く塩、こしょうをふって取り出す。足りなければさらに油少々を足して鶏肉、玉ねぎ、マッシュルームを順に炒め合わせ、塩、こしょうをふる。

8. ホワイトソースに、7、ゆでたマカロニを加えてよく混ぜる。

9. 耐熱皿に移し、チーズを散らし、230℃に温めたオーブンで15〜20分焼く。

Macaroni gratin

[Serves 4]

250g shrimp
1 boneless chicken thigh
1/2 onion
1 tin of mushrooms (100g)
100g macaroni
150g pizza cheese

[white sauce]
40g butter
50g flour
2 +1/2 cups (500ml) milk
1 cup (200ml) heavy cream
1/2-1 tsp salt
pepper

vegetable oil, salt,
  and pepper

[preparation] Heat the oven at 230°C.

1. Thinly slice the onion.
2. Remove the shells and devein the shrimp. Wash them well and wipe off the moisture thoroughly.
3. Cut the chicken into bite-sized pieces.
4. Drain the mushrooms.
5. Make the white sauce: Melt the butter in a frying pan, add the flour, and stir for 2-3 minutes. Make sure it doesn't burn. Pour in the milk gradually, and constantly stir for about 5 minutes until it thickens. Add the heavy cream and cook for a short time. Season with salt and pepper.
6. Boil the macaroni according to the time marked on the package. When it's done, drain it in a colander.
7. Heat the oil in a frying pan and stir-fry the shrimp. Season with a little salt and pepper. Empty them into a dish. Add a little more oil if necessary and stir-fry the chicken, onion, and mushrooms in this order, and season them with salt and pepper.
8. Add the chicken, onion, mushrooms, shrimps, and macaroni to the white sauce, and mix together.
9. Place it on a heat-resistant dish, sprinkle the cheese on top, and bake it in an oven at 230°C for 15-20 minutes.

揚げ鶏のねぎソース

Fried chicken with leek sauce

鶏肉が苦手だった父のためにつくった、わたしの思い出の一品です。数あるレシピの中でもいちばん人気のあるメニュー。カリッと上手に揚げる秘けつは、鶏肉を調理の前に冷蔵庫から出し、室温に戻すこと、下味の調味料の分量をきちんと守ることと、かたくり粉を揚げる直前にたっぷりとつけること。表面は色づいたのに中は生のまま…なんてことがないよう、二度揚げします。

This dish has a lot of memories for me, as I made this for my father who was not fond of chicken. This is one of the most popular dishes among my numerous recipes. The secrets to making crispy fried chicken are to take the chicken out of the fridge and bring it to room temperature before cooking, measure the exact amount of seasonings which are used for the chicken beforehand as instructed, and coat the chicken with plenty of potato starch just before frying it. Fry the chicken twice to avoid the center of the chicken being only half-cooked.

揚げ鶏のねぎソース

鶏もも肉　2枚
しょうゆ　大さじ1/2
酒　大さじ1/2
かたくり粉　適宜
揚げ油　適宜

［ねぎソース］
長ねぎ　1本
サラダ油　大さじ1/2
赤とうがらし（小口切り）　1本分
［合わせ調味料］
しょうゆ　カップ1/2（100ml）
酒　大さじ1
酢　大さじ2
砂糖　大さじ1+1/2

1. 鶏肉は室温に戻しておく。鶏肉の皮をフォークでところどころ刺し、半分に切って、しょうゆと酒につけておく。

2. ねぎソースをつくる。合わせ調味料を混ぜる。長ねぎは包丁で表面をところどころ刺すように切り込みを入れ、端から刻んでみじん切りにする。フライパンにサラダ油を熱し、長ねぎと赤とうがらしをサッと炒め、混ぜながら合わせ調味料を加えて火を止める。

3. 揚げ油を180℃に温める。鶏肉にかたくり粉をたっぷりとつけ、鶏肉を2〜3分揚げる。網にとり、約4分おいて余熱で火を通し、再び強火にして1〜2分揚げる。

4. 鶏肉の油をきり、食べやすい大きさに切る。皿に盛りつけ、ねぎソースをかける。

Fried chicken with leek sauce

[Serves 4]

2 chicken thighs
1/2 tbsp soy sauce
1/2 tbsp sake
potato starch for coating
oil for deep-frying

[leek sauce]
1 Japanese leek
1/2 tbsp vegetable oil
1 red chili pepper, chopped
[combined seasonings]
1/2 cup(100ml) soy sauce
1 tbsp sake
2 tbsp vinegar
1+1/2 tbsp sugar

1. Allow the chicken to reach room temperature before cooking. Pierce the chicken skin in several places with a fork, cut the chicken in half, and marinate in the soy sauce and sake.

2. Make the leek sauce: Mix the ingredients for the combined seasonings. Pierce the leek with the tip of a knife all over. Then, chop it finely starting from the end. Heat the oil in a frying pan. Stir-fry the leek and red chili. Stir constantly and add the combined seasonings. Turn off the heat.

3. Heat the oil to 180°C. Cover the chicken completely with potato starch. Deep-fry the chicken for 2-3 minutes. Put it on a rack and leave for about 4 minutes while it continues to cook with the residual heat. Then deep-fry it for 1-2 minutes over high heat again.

4. Drain and cut the chicken into bite-sized pieces. Place on a serving plate and pour the leek sauce over the top.

和風マーボー豆腐

Japanese-style *mabo-dofu*

わたしはマーボー豆腐が大好きです。この
マーボー豆腐は中国スープの代わりに和風
だしを使ってつくるやさしい味です。
豆腐を加える前の肉あんは冷凍しておける
ので、つくりおきしておくと食べたいときに
豆腐を加えるだけでできるので便利です。

I love *mabo-dofu*. This one uses Japanese-style dashi as a substitute for Chinese soup, giving it a mild flavor.
The meat *an*, before tofu is added,
freezes well. So it is convenient to keep
in the freezer. All you have to do is add
some tofu before eating.

和風マーボー豆腐

絹ごし豆腐　2丁（約700g）
合いびき肉　200g
にんにく（みじん切り）　大さじ1
しょうが（みじん切り）　大さじ1
長ねぎ（みじん切り）　大さじ4

［煮汁］
だし　カップ1+1/2（300ml）
しょうゆ　大さじ4〜5
みりん　大さじ2
砂糖　大さじ1

塩　少々
かたくり粉・水　各大さじ1
サラダ油　大さじ2
ごま油　適宜
赤とうがらし（小口切り）
　2〜3本分
粉ざんしょう　適宜

1. にんにく、しょうがは細かいみじん切りにする。
2. 長ねぎはみじん切りにする。
3. 豆腐は1.5cm角に切る。鍋にたっぷりの湯を沸かし、塩少々を入れて豆腐を入れ、約2分ゆでてざるに上げる。
4. かたくり粉は同量の水で溶いておく。
5. 煮汁の材料を鍋に合わせ、温めておく。
6. フライパンにサラダ油を熱し、にんにく、しょうが、長ねぎを炒め、香りが出たら合いびき肉を炒める。肉に火が通ったら煮汁を入れ、再び煮立ったら水溶きかたくり粉でとろみをつける。豆腐を加えて軽く混ぜ合わせ、ごま油を回しかける。
7. 器に盛り、好みで赤とうがらしの小口切りや粉ざんしょうをふる。

Japanese-style *mabo-dofu*

[Serves 4]

2 packs soft tofu
(approx.700g)

200g ground beef
and pork mixture

1 tbsp garlic
(finely chopped)

1 tbsp ginger
(finely chopped)

4 tbsp Japanese leek
(finely chopped)

[sauce]

1+1/2cups (300ml) dashi

4-5 tbsp soy sauce

2 tbsp mirin

1 tbsp sugar

salt

1 tbsp potato starch

1 tbsp water

2 tbsp vegetable oil

sesame oil

2-3 red chili peppers(chopped)

sansho powder --- for garnish

1. Finely chop the garlic and ginger.

2. Chop up the Japanese leek.

3. Cut the tofu into 1.5cm cubes. Bring a pot of water to a boil, add a little salt, and boil the tofu in it for about 2 minutes before pouring it into a colander.

4. Dissolve the potato starch in an equal amount of water.

5. Combine the ingredients for the sauce in a pan and heat it.

6. Heat the vegetable oil in a frying pan and stir-fry the garlic, ginger and Japanese leek. Once they become fragrant, stir-fry the ground beef and pork mixture. When the meat is cooked through, pour the sauce in and when it comes to a boil, add the dissolved potato starch and let it thicken. Add the tofu, and mix gently. Sprinkle sesame oil around the edge of the pan.

7. Serve on a plate, garnish with slices of red chili pepper or *sansho* powder if preferred.

牛肉コロッケ

Beef and potato croquettes

玉ねぎと牛肉をバターで炒め、肉汁ごとじゃがいも
に加えて、その香りやうまみを生かします。食感を
残すために、玉ねぎは少し大きめに切り、炒めす
ぎないようにしてください。
じゃがいもが主役の料理なので、じゃがいもがおい
しい季節や、買っても新しいうちにつくってみてくだ
さい。男爵など、ホクホクした種類がおすすめです。

Cook the onion and beef with butter, and add
them to the potatoes along with the gravy so as
to transfer their flavor and aroma to the potatoes.
The onion should not be cut too finely, nor should
it be over-cooked. This will help to ensure that
you can still appreciate the texture of the onion.
As potatoes are a main feature of this dish, try
this recipe when potatoes are in season or use
fresh potatoes from the store. I particularly
recommend soft-textured potatoes such as the
Danshaku variety.

牛肉コロッケ

【 材料 20コ分 】

じゃがいも　4コ（500g）
玉ねぎ　1コ（200g）
牛切り落とし肉　200g
塩・こしょう　各適宜
バター　30g

[衣]
小麦粉・溶き卵・パン粉　各適宜

揚げ油　適宜

[キャベツのコールスローサラダ]
キャベツ（せん切り）　200g
レモン汁　大さじ1
オリーブ油　大さじ2
塩・こしょう　各少々

[ソース]
とんかつソース　大さじ3
トマトケチャップ　大さじ2

マスタード　適宜

1. じゃがいもは皮をむいて4〜6等分に切って水にさらし、水けをきる。耐熱ボウルに紙タオルを敷き、じゃがいもを入れる。ふんわりとラップをし、電子レンジ（600W）で柔らかくなるまで5〜6分かける。

2. ラップを外し、紙タオルを取ってじゃがいもが熱いうちにつぶす。

 * 電子レンジを使用せずに、鍋でゆでる場合は106ページを参照。

3. 玉ねぎは1cm角に切る。牛肉は2cm角に切る。フライパンにバターを熱し、牛肉を炒める。玉ねぎを加えて炒め、塩小さじ1/2、こしょう少々をふる。

4. つぶしたじゃがいもに炒めた牛肉と玉ねぎを肉汁ごと加える。塩、こしょうで味を調え、よく混ぜ合わせる。

5. 食べやすい大きさに丸め、小麦粉、溶き卵、パン粉の順に衣をつける。170℃の油でカリッとするまで揚げる。コールスローサラダの材料を混ぜ、コロッケとともに器に盛り、ソースとマスタードを添える。

Beef and potato croquettes

[Makes 20]

4 potatoes (500g)

1 onion (200g)

200g beef trimmings

salt and pepper
--- to taste

30g butter

[coating]

flour, beaten eggs,
breadcrumbs

vegetable oil
for deep-flying

[coleslaw]

200g shredded cabbage

1 tbsp lemon juice

2 tbsp olive oil

salt and pepper

[sauce]

3 tbsp *tonkatsu* sauce

2 tbsp tomato ketchup

mustard

1. Peel and cut each potato into 4-6 pieces. Soak them in water and drain. Line a microwave-resistant bowl with some paper towel and add the potatoes. Cover loosely with plastic wrap and microwave for 5-6 minutes until tender.

2. Remove the plastic wrap and paper towel from the bowl. Mash the potatoes while they are hot.

 * If you want to boil in a pot instead of using a microwave, see page 107.

3. Cut the onion into 1cm square pieces. Cut the beef into 2cm square pieces. Heat the butter in the frying pan and stir-fry the beef. Add the onions and continue to stir-fry. Season with 1/2 tsp salt and a little pepper.

4. Add the beef mixture and juices to the mashed potatoes. Season to taste with salt and pepper and mix well.

5. Shape into balls. Coat with flour, beaten egg, and then breadcrumbs. Deep-fry at 170 °C until crispy. Mix the ingredients of the coleslaw, and put onto a plate along with the croquettes. Serve with sauce and mustard.

豚カツ

"Tonkatsu" (pork cutlets)

豚カツは豚肉にパン粉をつけて揚げたもの。豚カツをつくる日は、わたしはいつもその日食べる分と一緒に、急なお友達用として冷凍庫に常備しておくためにたくさんつくります。

大きいものから一口サイズのものまで、大きさをいろいろ変えてつくっておくと、気分や料理に合わせて使い分けられるので便利です。豚カツとして食べるときは、どんと大きいのを1枚揚げて豪快な盛りつけに。一方、カツ丼は煮汁を含んだカツの衣がおいしいので、一口大に揚げたカツでつくることもあります。

"Tonkatsu" is deep-fried breaded pork. When I cook "tonkatsu," I always make much more than my family can eat on that day and store the rest in the freezer for unexpected visits from friends. If you prepare various sizes of "tonkatsu" from bite-size to large cutlets, they can be used for a variety of recipes according to your needs. To make "tonkatsu", I use a whole cutlet and place it boldly on a plate. But when I make "katsu-don", I sometimes use bite-sized "tonkatsu", because the extra breading absorbs the soup and makes it tastier.

豚 カ ツ

豚肩ロース肉　1kg
　　または2cm厚さのもの　4枚
塩・こしょう　各少々

［ 衣 ］
小麦粉・溶き卵・パン粉　各適宜

キャベツ　1/2コ
揚げ油　適宜
とんかつソース　適宜
和がらし　適宜
レモン　適宜

1. キャベツはせん切りにし、氷水にさらしてパリッとさせる。水けをきってポリ袋へ入れ、食べる直前まで冷蔵庫で冷やしておく。
2. 豚肉は2cm厚さに切る。揚げたときに縮まないように脂肪と赤身の間の筋に包丁で切り込みを入れ、塩、こしょうをふる。
3. 小麦粉をまぶして溶き卵にくぐらせ、パン粉をつける。
4. 揚げ油を170℃に熱し、3を揚げる。表面がきつね色になり、中まで火が通ったら余分な油をきる。
5. 一口大に切り分け、キャベツのせん切り、好みのソース、和がらしを添える。レモンと塩で食べてもおいしい。

"Tonkatsu" (pork cutlets)

[Serves 4]

1kg or 4 slices (2cm-thick) pork shoulder loin
salt and pepper

[coating]
flour, beaten eggs, breadcrumbs

1/2 head cabbage
oil for deep-frying
tonkatsu sauce
Japanese mustard
lemon

1. Shred the cabbage and soak in ice water to make it crispy. Drain, put it in a plastic bag, and chill in the refrigerator until serving.
2. Slice the pork into about 2cm-thick slices. Slash the sinew running between the fat and lean tissue with a knife in order to prevent it from shrinking when deep-fried. Season with salt and pepper.
3. Dust the pork slices with flour, dip them in beaten eggs, and coat them with breadcrumbs.
4. Heat the oil to 170°C. Deep-fry the pork until golden brown on the outside and cooked through. Drain off excess oil.
5. Cut the fried pork into bite-sized pieces. Serve with the cabbage, your favorite sauce, and Japanese mustard. It's also tasty with just lemon and salt.

さ ば の み そ 煮

Mackerel simmered in miso

家庭料理の定番ですが、あっさりめのみそ
味なので、白いご飯だけでなく、パンにもよ
く合います。わたしはワインを飲みたいときに
はガーリックトーストと一緒に食べています。
さばは、大きく切るより、小さめに切るほう
が飽きずに最後までおいしく食べられます。

This is one of the most popular and basic
dishes in Japanese home cooking. However, my version is cooked with light miso
sauce, which goes well with bread as well
as with white steamed rice. When I feel
like drinking wine, I lay slices of garlic
bread along with this on my plate.
I like to cut the mackerel into small pieces rather than large ones. That way, I can
savor each bite.

さばのみそ煮

【 材料 4人分 】

さば　1匹（正味400g）
しょうが　1かけ
酒　カップ1/2（100ml）
水　カップ1/2（100ml）
砂糖　大さじ3
しょうゆ　大さじ1
みりん　大さじ4
みそ　大さじ5〜6

1. まず、さばを三枚におろす。頭を切り落とし（a）、包丁の先で腹を切り開いて内臓を取り除く。よく洗って紙タオルでふく。包丁を水平に保ち、背骨に沿って尾のほうから切って上身を切り離す（b）。裏返して反対側も同様にする。腹骨をすき取る（c）。切り身はそれぞれ3等分のそぎ切りにする。

   * 「三枚におろす」とは、切り身が2枚と骨のことを指す（d）。

2. しょうがは皮をむいて薄切りにする。

3. 鍋に酒と水を入れて火にかけ、アルコール分をとばしてから砂糖、しょうゆ、みりん、みそを加えて混ぜる。煮立ったら、さばを並べ入れる。しょうがを加え、煮汁が再び煮立ったら落としぶたをし、弱火にして10〜15分煮る。

4. 煮汁が少なくなり、とろみがつけば完成。器に盛り、しょうがと一緒に煮汁をかける。

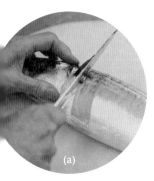(a)
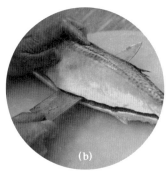(b)
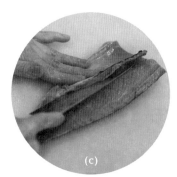(c)

Mackerel simmered in miso

[Serves 4]

1 mackerel
(400g in fillets)
1 knob ginger
1/2 cup(100ml) sake
1/2 cup(100ml) water
3 tbsp sugar
1 tbsp soy sauce
4 tbsp mirin
5-6 tbsp miso

1. First, fillet the mackerel into three pieces: Cut off the head(a). Slice the stomach open with the tip of the knife and remove the innards. Wash thoroughly and wipe dry with a paper towel. Then, keeping the knife flat, cut horizontally from the tail along the side of the spine to loosen the top fillet(b). Turn it over and repeat on the other side. Shave off the bones around the stomach(c). Cut each fillet into three equal pieces in *sogi-giri*(diagonal-cut).

   * "Fillet a fish into three pieces" means two pieces of flesh and one of bone.(d)

2. Peel the ginger and thinly slice it.

3. Put the sake and water in a pan and turn on the heat. When the alcohol has boiled off, add sugar, soy sauce, mirin and miso into the pan and mix. When it comes to a boil, place the mackerel in the pan. Add the ginger. When the sauce comes to a boil again, put a drop-lid on and simmer for 10-15 minutes over low heat.

4. When the sauce is reduced and becomes syrupy, it is done. Arrange on a plate and pour the sauce on top with ginger slices.

(d)

銀だらの香り煮

Aromatic stewed sablefish

煮魚は和食の中でも少しむずかしいと思われるようですが、これはとても簡単なのでぜひ試してみてください。この煮つけのたれの割合を覚えておけば、ほかの魚でも同じようにつくれます。
生の春菊とわかめの上に熱い煮汁をかけると、思いがけないおいしさです。

People often seem to think that cooking *nizakana* (simmering fish with broth) is a bit difficult compared to other Japanese dishes. But this is a very easy recipe. So, I'd like you to try it. Once you learn the balance of the ingredients for the broth, you can cook it with other fish as well.
The hot broth poured over raw *shungiku* and wakame turns this into an unexpected delicacy.

銀 だ ら の 香 り 煮

銀だら　4〜5切れ（450〜500g）

[調味料]
しょうゆ　大さじ4
砂糖　大さじ2
酒　大さじ4
みりん　大さじ4
みそ　小さじ1
豆板醤（トーバンジャン）　小さじ1〜2

にんにく（みじん切り）　大さじ1
しょうが（みじん切り）　大さじ1
長ねぎ（粗みじん切り）　1/2本分
春菊　適宜
わかめ（戻したもの）　適宜

1. 春菊は葉先を摘み、氷水に入れてパリッとさせ水けをよくきる。
2. わかめは食べやすい大きさに切り、春菊と合わせて皿に盛りつけ、冷蔵庫で冷やしておく。
3. 銀だらは水けをふいて、1切れを半分に切る。
4. 鍋に調味料を合わせて煮立て、銀だらを重ならないように並べ入れる。
5. 再び煮立ったら、にんにく、しょうが、長ねぎを加え、落としぶたをして弱火で10分ほど煮る。
6. 銀だらを2にのせ、煮汁をかける。

Aromatic stewed sablefish

[Serves 4]

4-5 fillets sablefish
   (450 ~ 500g)

[seasonings]
4 tbsp soy sauce
2 tbsp sugar
4 tbsp sake
4 tbsp mirin
1 tsp miso
1-2 tsp *To-Ban-Jan*

1 tbsp minced garlic
1 tbsp minced ginger
1/2 Japanese leek, chopped
shungiku
   (chrysanthemum greens),
wakame seaweed
   --- to serve

1. Separate the leaves from the stems of the *shungiku*, and crisp the leaves by soaking in ice water, and drain well.
2. Cut the wakame into bite-sized pieces. Mix the *shungiku* and wakame, and put it on a serving plate. Cool it in a refrigerator
3. Pat dry the sablefish. Cut each fillet in half.
4. Combine the seasonings in a pan, and bring it to a boil. Add the fish, making sure you don't put the pieces on top of each other.
5. When it comes to a boil again, add the garlic, ginger, and leek. Put a drop-lid on and simmer for about 10 minutes over low heat.
6. Place the sablefish on top of the *shungiku* and wakame, and pour the piping hot sauce on top.

さけとえびのつくね

Salmon and shrimp
tsukune meatballs

海外に行くと、さけとえびが好きな人が
多いのに驚きます。この料理は海外で思
いついた一品。焼き鳥のようにしたり、ハ
ンバーガーにしてもおいしく食べられます。

Every time I go abroad, I am always
amazed at how much people love salmon and shrimp. This is a recipe I came
up with when I was abroad. They are
also tasty in skewers like yakitori or as
patties for hamburgers.

さけとえびのつくね

生さけ　3切れ（300g）
むきえび　10匹（200g）
玉ねぎ　1/2コ（100g）
酒　大さじ1
塩・こしょう　各少々
サラダ油　少々
すだち（半分に切る）　適宜
粉ざんしょう　適宜

[レモンポン酢]
みりん　カップ1/2（100ml）
しょうゆ　カップ1/2（100ml）
レモン汁　大さじ4
昆布（5cm角）　1枚

[甘辛だれ]
しょうゆ　カップ1/4（50ml）
みりん　カップ1/4（50ml）
砂糖　大さじ2

1. さけは皮と骨を除き、粗く刻んでから包丁でたたく。

2. えびは洗い、背ワタを取る。粗く刻んでからたたく。尾の部分は細かくたたき、身の部分は食感が残る程度にたたく。

3. 玉ねぎは7〜8mm角に切る。

4. ボウルにたたいたさけ、えびを入れ、酒、塩、こしょうを加えて混ぜ合わせる。玉ねぎを入れてさらに混ぜ合わせる。

5. 4を5cmの円形に形づくる。フライパンにサラダ油を熱し、焼いて中まで火を通す。

6. レモンポン酢をつくる。昆布は水でサッと洗って水けをふく。鍋にみりんを入れて火にかけ、煮立ったら弱火にし、2〜3分煮詰める。ボウルに移し、しょうゆ、レモン汁、昆布を加えて冷蔵庫で保存する。

7. 甘辛だれをつくる。小鍋に調味料を合わせて火にかける。煮立ったら弱火にして約5分、少しとろみがつくくらいまで煮詰める。

8. 器に盛り、すだち、粉ざんしょう、レモンポン酢、甘辛だれを添える。

Salmon and shrimp *tsukune* meatballs

[Makes 10]

---

3 salmon fillets (300g)
10 shelled shrimp (200g)
1/2 onion (100g)
1 tbsp sake
salt and pepper
vegetable oil
sudachi (halved)
  --- to serve
sansho powder

[lemon *ponzu* sauce]
1/2 cup (100ml) mirin
1/2 cup (100ml) soy sauce
4 tbsp lemon juice
5cm-square-piece
  kombu kelp

[salty-sweet sauce]
1/4 cup (50ml) soy sauce
1/4 cup (50ml) mirin
2 tbsp suger

1. Remove the skin and bones from the salmon. Chop it coarsely first and then mince it.
2. Wash the shrimp and devein them. Chop it coarsely first and then mince it. Mince the tail completely and mince the body rather coarsely so that the texture remains.
3. Cut the onion into 7-8mm squares.
4. Put the salmon and shrimp in a bowl, add the sake, salt, and pepper, and mix. Add the onion and mix.
5. Shape the mixture into 5cm rounds. Pan-fry them until they are cooked through.
6. Make lemon *ponzu* sauce: Rinse the kombu lightly with water and wipe it dry. Put the mirin in a pan and bring it to a boil. Turn down the heat and simmer for a couple of minutes. Transfer the mirin to a bowl and add the soy sauce, lemon juice, and kombu. Keep in the refrigerator.
7. Make the salty-sweet sauce: Combine the ingredients in a small pan, and heat. When it comes to a boil, turn down the heat to low heat and let it simmer for about 5 minutes until it thickens a little.
8. Serve the *tsukune* with sudachi, *sansho* powder, lemon *ponzu* sauce and salty-sweet sauce.

さけの南蛮づけ

Deep-fried salmon marinated
in *nanbanzu*

南蛮づけとは、材料を油で揚げ、赤とうが
らしなどと一緒に酢づけにしたもの。野菜
もたくさん食べたいので、たっぷりの野菜
と一緒につけ込みます。
一年を通してつくっていますが、冬にはゆず、
夏はすだちやレモンなど、そのときどきで手
に入るかんきつ類を使い、香りを楽しみます。

Nanbanzuke is a dish in which ingredients are deep-fried and then marinated
in vinegared sauce with red peppers.
Because I want to eat lots of vegetables, I
use plenty of them in this recipe.
I cook this dish throughout the year, and
use seasonal citrus fruits, such as yuzu
in winter and sudachi or lemons in summer, to enjoy their fragrance.

さけの南蛮づけ

生ざけ（切り身）　4切れ（400g）
にんじん　小1本（100g）
玉ねぎ　1/2コ（100g）
セロリ　1/2本（正味80g）
しょうが　小1かけ
赤とうがらし（小口切り）　2本分
ゆず　適宜
小麦粉　大さじ3
塩・こしょう　各少々
揚げ油　適宜

［南蛮酢］
だし　カップ1（200ml）
うす口しょうゆ　大さじ3
酢　カップ3/4（150ml）
砂糖　大さじ4
塩　少々

1. にんじんは4〜5cm長さのせん
   切りにする。

2. 玉ねぎは薄切りにする。

3. セロリは筋を取って4〜5cm長さ
   のせん切りにする。

4. しょうがもせん切りにする。

5. ボウルにだし、うす口しょうゆ、酢、
   砂糖、塩を合わせ、南蛮酢をつくる。

 * 好みでゆずやレモン、すだちなど
   の果汁大さじ1を加えてもよい。

6. さけは食べやすい大きさに切る。
   塩、こしょうをふり、全体に小麦
   粉をまぶし、170〜180℃の揚げ
   油で揚げる。熱いうちに南蛮酢
   につけ、にんじん、玉ねぎ、セロ
   リ、しょうが、赤とうがらしを加え、
   ゆずの皮をのせて香りをつける。
   ラップをし、冷蔵庫に入れて味を
   なじませる。

Deep-fried salmon marinated in *nanbanzu*

[Serves 4]

4 salmon fillets (400g)
1 small carrot (100g)
1/2 onion (100g)
1/2 stalk celery (80g)
1 small knob ginger
2 red chili peppers, chopped
yuzu
3 tbsp flour
salt and pepper
vegetable oil for deep-frying

[*nanbanzu* sauce]
1 cup(200ml) dashi
3 tbsp light soy sauce
3/4 cup(150ml) vinegar
4 tbsp sugar
salt

1. Cut the carrot into 4-5cm thin strips.
2. Slice the onion.
3. String the celery and cut it into 4-5cm thin strips.
4. Cut the ginger into thin strips.
5. Combine the dashi, light soy sauce, vinegar, sugar, and salt in a bowl, and mix them to make the *nanbanzu* sauce.
   * You can add 1 tbsp juice of citrus such as yuzu, lemon, or sudachi if preferred.
6. Cut the salmon into bite-sized pieces. Sprinkle salt and pepper over the salmon and cover the salmon completely with flour. Deep-fry the salmon in oil at 170-180°C. Marinate the salmon in *nanbanzu* while they are hot. Add the carrot, onion, celery, ginger, red chili pepper and top it with yuzu zest for fragrance. Cover with plastic wrap and put in the refrigerator. Let it stand for a while to marinate.

えびカツ
Ebikatsu (shrimp cutlets)

小さいえびは、そのままフライにするより、一つにまと
めて大きなカツにすると、食べごたえもあり、見た目も
おいしさも歯ざわりも変わります。えびは火が通りす
ぎないように揚げましょう。わが家ではパーティーのと
きにいつも揚げたてのアツアツを出しています。

Small shrimp better satisfy your hunger and have
a more appealing look, taste and texture when they
are deep-fried together in a cutlet than fried separately. Be careful not to overcook the shrimp. I always serve this dish sizzing hot at my home parties.

えびカツ

えび　24匹

小麦粉　大さじ6

溶き卵　1コ分

水　大さじ1

パン粉　適宜

[タルタルソース]

きゅうりのピクルス　大さじ3
　（みじん切り）

ゆで卵（みじん切り）　2コ分

玉ねぎ（みじん切り）　1/4コ分
　（大さじ3）

マヨネーズ　カップ1（200ml）

牛乳　大さじ1〜2

和がらし　少々

塩・こしょう　各適宜

揚げ油　適宜

レモン　適宜

1. タルタルソースをつくる。ボウルにマヨネーズを入れ、牛乳で溶きのばし、和がらしを加えて混ぜる。ピクルス、ゆで卵、玉ねぎを加えて混ぜ、塩、こしょうで味を調える。

2. 小麦粉に溶き卵、分量の水を混ぜ合わせ、ペースト状にする。

3. えびは殻と尾を取り除き、つまようじで背ワタを引き抜く。長さを半分に切り、6切れを1コ分としてまとめる。円く形を整え、塩・こしょう各少々で下味をつける。

4. 3をターナーなどですくって2を表面にぬり、パン粉をまぶす。

5. 180〜190℃の油で揚げて中まで火を通す。

6. 器に盛り、好みのソース、タルタルソース、レモンを添える。

Ebikatsu (shrimp cutlets)

24 shrimp
6 tbsp flour
1 egg, beaten
1 tbsp water
breadcrumbs

[tartar sauce]
3 tbsp pickled cucumber,
  finely chopped
2 boiled eggs,
  finely chopped
1/4 finely chopped onion(3 tbsp)
1 cup (200ml) mayonnaise
1-2 tbsp milk
Japanese mustard

salt and pepper
vegetable oil
  for deep-frying
lemon

1. Make the tartar sauce: Put the mayonnaise in a bowl, and dilute it with the milk. Add a little Japanese mustard, and mix. Mix in the pickled cucumber, egg, and onion. Season to taste with salt and pepper.

2. Mix the flour, beaten egg, and 1 tbsp water until the mixture becomes paste-like.

3. Remove the shells and tails from the shrimp. Devein them with a toothpick. Cut the shrimp in half. Use 6 pieces per portion to make round, tight, flat patties, and season with salt and pepper.

4. Scoop the patties using a turner and spread the paste made in step 2 over the surface. Then coat the patties with breadcrumbs.

5. Deep-fry the patties in oil at 180-190°C until they are cooked through.

6. Serve with your favorite sauce, tartar sauce, and lemon.

さくら ｜ Sakura

さくら

春に咲く桜は、わたしの大好きな花です。

日本人はもちろん、今では外国の人も愛する花だと思います。

日一日と暖かくなり、本格的な春の訪れが近くなってくると、毎年、

桜の開花ニュースが待ち遠しくなります。開花したと思ったら、

10日ほどで散ってしまう、いさぎよくもはかない花。

なのに、なぜか人の心をなごませてくれます。

桜の季節は、玄関や部屋のところどころに桜を飾ってみたり、

飾った花から一輪摘んでお酒やお茶にすっと浮かべてみたり。

ときには、枝を小さく折ってはし置きにして楽しんでいます。

桜のモチーフをつけた器や布なども、

今ではたくさん集まりました。

春は四季の中でいちばん好きな季節。

おいしい魚や野菜がたくさん出回り、

とりわけ香りのいい葉物がわたしの料理づくりの意欲をかきたてます。

日本に生まれてよかった、日本人でよかった。

この豊かな、やさしい季節の一日を

大事に過ごさなければ、と思います。

Sakura

Spring in Japan reminds me of sakura (cherry blossoms),
my favorite flower.
Sakura are now widely loved by many people in the world,
and not only by Japanese people.
When it gets warmer and spring feels like it's just around the corner,
I am anxious for the news that cherry-blossoms are in bloom.
Once cherry blossoms have fully opened,
the petals soon fall to the ground.
They only last for about ten days after the buds have bloomed.
They are gracious and, though very fragile,
the blossoms somehow soothe people's minds.
During cherry-blossom season,
I put some cherry blossoms in the hallway or
in the rooms of my home for decoration, or pick some petals
and set them nicely afloat on a cup of Japanese sake or green tea.
Sometimes, I pick a tiny twig off a sakura tree
and place it on the table as a chopstick rest.
I now have many kinds of tableware or tablecloths with
cherry-blossom motifs on them.
Spring is my favorite season of the year.
Many delicious fish and vegetables become available in the market.
When I see sweet-smelling herbs or fresh leafy vegetables,
it arouses in me a feeling of enthusiasm for cooking.
I am happy to be born in Japan, and I am enjoying living here.
I like to cherish every moment of this rich
and generous season of the year.

本書で使われている主な調味料
Basic ingredients used in this book

しょうゆ Soy sause

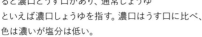

大豆を原料とした日本の代表的な調味料。塩味と独特のうまみがあり、日本料理に不可欠なもの。うまみがあって香りが高く、そのままつけて食べるほか、煮物、たれなど、幅広く使われる。さまざまな種類があるが、大きく分けると濃口とうす口があり、通常しょうゆといえば濃口しょうゆを指す。濃口はうす口に比べ、色は濃いが塩分は低い。

The soy-based sauce essential for Japanese recipes contains salt and has a uniquely savory taste. It is widely used as dipping sauce, for seasoning simmered food, and for adding flavor to Japanese-style sauces. There are various kinds of soy sauce, with regular soy sauce (*koikuchi*) offering darker color and less salt compared with light soy sauce (*usukuchi*).

うす口しょうゆ Light soy sauce

材料の持ち味や色を生かすため、色や香りを抑え、塩分を強くしたしょうゆ。関西地方を中心に使われている。淡い色の野菜や白身魚を煮るときや、吸物の汁にあまり色をつけたくないときに使われる。塩分はしょうゆの中でいちばん高い。

This soy sauce, which is favored in the Kansai area, has moderate color and flavor but is saltier than regular soy sauce. Light soy sauce is in fact the saltiest of all soy sauce varieties. Harmonizing with the natural flavor and color of ingredients, it is used for simmering pale-colored vegetables or white fish, and for seasoning clear soups.

穀物酢 *Kokumotsu-su* (Rice and grain vinegar)

日本の家庭で使われている代表的な酢。米や小麦、酒かす、コーンなどからつくられる。さっぱりとした酸味が特徴で和食だけでなく、洋食や中国料理など幅広く使われる。ワインビネガーなどと比べ、酸度は4.2％前後と低い。

This is the most commonly used vinegar in Japanese homes. It is made from a blend of grains such as rice, wheat, and corn and sake lees. It has a savory and sour flavor, and is widely used for not just Japanese but Western and Chinese dishes. Compared to wine vinegar, it has less acidity at 4.2 %.

料理酒 *Ryori-shu* (Cooking sake)

料理用に使われる酒。飲むための日本酒と異なり、酸味や雑味があるが、これが肉や魚の生臭みを消したり、料理にコクやうまみを与える。商品によって塩や甘味料などが添加されているものもある。普通の日本酒でも代用可。

This is sake used for cooking. Unlike the sake for drinking, the cooking sake is a little sour and has a bit of an undesirable taste but it helps to remove the unpleasant smell of fish and meat, and gives deeper flavor to dishes. Some products have added salt or sugar etc. You can substitute it with ordinary sake for drinking.

みりん Mirin

焼酎に蒸したもち米と米こうじを加えて熟成させた甘みのある酒。料理に甘みをつけたり、つやを出したりするときに使う。砂糖と違って甘さがマイルドで、うまみ成分も含まれる。また、みりんに含まれるアルコール分には、煮くずれを防いだり、肉や魚の臭みを消したりする働きもある。

Sweet alcoholic liquid produced from distilled spirits, steamed glutinous rice, and malted rice. Mirin adds sweetness and luster to ingredients. Compared with sugar, mirin offers a milder sweetness and flavor. The alcohol contained in the mirin protects simmered ingredients from crumbling and also removes the smell of meat and fish.

みそ Miso

大豆を主原料とし、米や麦を加えて発酵させてつくる日本古来の調味料。地域により味、色、香りが異なり、その種類は数百とも言われている。本書では特に断りがない限り、黄色みを帯びた淡色の米みそを使用している。

Traditional Japanese seasoning produced from fermented soybeans, rice, and wheat. There are several hundred regional variations in taste, color, and flavor of miso paste. In this book, I use rice miso (komemiso), which has a yellowish color, except in cases where I suggest using other specific miso pastes.

上白糖 Johakuto (Refined white sugar)

日本の家庭料理で最も使われている砂糖。レシピで砂糖と書かれている場合は、ほとんどが上白糖を指す。日本特有の砂糖で、グラニュー糖より結晶が細かく、しっとりとしている。クセがなく、水に溶けやすいのが特徴。

This is the sugar most commonly used in Japanese homes. If the recipe says "sugar", it usually implies this sugar. It is unique to Japan and has finer crystals than granulated sugar and contains some moisture. It has no strong flavor and dissolves easily.

鶏ガラスープの素 Granulated Chinese chicken soup stock

鶏ガラのエキスをベースに、野菜のエキスで風味づけされたもの。中国料理向けのインスタント調味料。スープのベースにするほか、炒め物などにも使われる。

Ready-made seasoning produced from the essence of chicken soup stock and flavored with vegetable essence. It is mainly used for Chinese recipes such as soups and sautéed dishes.

とんかつソース Tonkatsu sauce

豚カツ専用につくられたソースで、イギリスのウースター市のソースに似せてつくられたウスターソースの仲間。ウスターソースより甘みが強く、どろりとしている。

This Japanese sauce is mainly used for deep-fried pork (tonkatsu) and it imitates England's famous Worcester sauce. Although it is a kind of Worcester sauce, tonkatsu sauce is sweeter and thicker than other Japanese-style Worcester sauces.

ごま油 Sesame oil

ごまを圧搾してとる油。一般的に、ごまを香ばしくいってから搾るので、色は褐色で、ごまの独特な芳香がある。

Made from compressed sesame seeds. Regular sesame oil is made from toasted sesame seeds and is brown in color with a strong flavor.

豆板醤 To-Ban-Jan

中国料理の調味料の一種で、四川料理で多く使われる。ピリッとした辛みとうまみがあり、炒め物、煮物、あんかけなどの料理の辛みづけに利用する。

Chinese chili paste mainly used for Sichuan-style recipes. To-Ban-Jan is used to add spiciness and a savory taste to sautéed dishes, simmered dishes, and thick liquid starch sauces.

かたくり粉 Potato starch (Katakuri ko)

一般に出回っているのはじゃがいものでんぷん。本来は、かたくりの地下茎からとったでんぷんのことで、名前もそこからきている。揚げ物の衣やとろみづけに使う。とろみづけに使う場合は、ダマにならないようにあらかじめ水に溶いてから加える。

Traditional Japanese katakuri ko used to be made from the root of katakuri, and was named after the plant. Today, starch made from potato is available as a substitute for katakuri ko. Potato starch is used for deep-fried batter and as a thickener of soups and sauces. When using it as a thickener, dissolve it in water before use so that it does not become lumpy.

2

VEGETABLES

野菜のおかず

にんじんと
ツナのサラダ

Carrot and tuna salad

にんじんがたくさん余ったとき、持っていた
材料だけでつくってみたのがこのサラダ。も
う30年以上つくり続けていますが、いまだ
に人気のあるレシピです。
にんじんはゆでるのでもなく、生でもなく、電
子レンジにかけます。玉ねぎとにんにくを細
かくみじん切りにするのがポイントです。

When I had a lot of carrots left unused I
came up with this salad recipe, using other
ingredients that I had in my kitchen. I first
introduced this recipe more than 30 years
ago, but it is still quite popular.
The carrots are not boiled, nor eaten raw.
They are microwaved. The key to this recipe is to finely chop the onion and garlic.

にんじんとツナのサラダ

【 材料 4人分 】

にんじん　250g
玉ねぎ（細かいみじん切り）　大さじ2
にんにく（細かいみじん切り）　小さじ1
サラダ油
　　またはオリーブ油　大さじ1
ツナ缶　小1/2缶（30g）

［ドレッシング］
白ワインビネガー　大さじ1
粒マスタード　大さじ1
レモン汁　大さじ1
塩・こしょう　各適宜

1. にんじんは5～6cm長さのせん
   切りにする。耐熱ボウルに入れ、
   玉ねぎ、にんにく、サラダ油を加
   えて混ぜる。
2. ラップでふんわりと覆い、電子レ
   ンジ（600W）に1分10秒～1分20
   秒かける。
3. 電子レンジからボウルを取り出し、
   ラップを外す。軽く混ぜ合わせ、
   汁けをきったツナ、ドレッシング
   の材料を順に加えて混ぜる。
4. 冷蔵庫で冷やしてドレッシングを
   なじませる。

Carrot and tuna salad

250g carrot
2 tbsp onion, finely chopped
1 tsp garlic, finely chopped
1 tbsp vegetable oil
   or olive oil
1/2 small can of tuna(30g)

[dressing]
1 tbsp white wine vinegar
1 tbsp grain mustard
1 tbsp lemon juice
salt and pepper --- to taste

1. Cut the carrot into 5-6cm thin strips. Put them in a microwave-resistant bowl and mix in the onion, garlic, and oil.

2. Cover it loosely with plastic wrap and microwave at 600W for 1 minute and 10 to 20 seconds.

3. Remove the bowl from the microwave and remove the wrap. Mix lightly and add the drained tuna and the dressing ingredients. Mix together.

4. Chill in the refrigerator to allow the dressing to soak into the vegetables.

ポテトサラダ

Potato salad

ポテトサラダにはたくさんのバリエーションがありますが、これがいちばんシンプルで日本中のどの家庭でも食べている味です。どこの国でも手に入る材料なので、いつでもどこでもつくれます。きゅうりは少し厚めに切って食感を残すこと、玉ねぎは水にさらしすぎないで、マヨネーズを加えるときにふわっと混ぜることがおいしくつくるコツです。

There are many variations of potato salad recipes, but this one is the simplest, most basic taste enjoyed in home cooking across Japan. The ingredients are easily available in any country, so you can make it any time, anywhere. The tip to making it delicious is to slice the cucumbers slightly thick for crispy texture, not to soak the sliced onions in the water for too long, and to fold in the mayonnaise gently.

ポテトサラダ

じゃがいも
　4〜5コ（450g）

きゅうり　1本

玉ねぎ　小1/2コ

ハム　2枚

マヨネーズ
　大さじ5〜6

塩・こしょう　各適宜

1. じゃがいもは皮をむいて4〜6等分に切って水にさらし、水けをきる。耐熱ボウルに紙タオルを敷き、じゃがいもを入れる。ふんわりとラップをし、電子レンジ（600W）で柔らかくなるまで5〜6分かける。

2. ラップを外し、紙タオルを取ってじゃがいもが熱いうちにつぶし、冷ましておく。

   ＊ 鍋でゆでる場合は、以下のようにゆでること。じゃがいもは皮つきのままよく洗い、丸ごと鍋に入れてかぶるまで水を注ぎ、ふたをして火にかける。煮立ったら弱火にして20〜25分、柔らかくなるまでゆでる。熱いうちに皮をむいてボウルに入れ、つぶす。

3. きゅうりは薄切りにし、塩をまぶして5分おく。しんなりしたら水けを絞る。

4. 玉ねぎは薄切りにし、水に5分さらしてから水けを絞る。

5. ハムは半分にし、1cm幅に切る。

6. きゅうり、玉ねぎ、ハムを、つぶしたじゃがいもに加えて混ぜ合わせる。マヨネーズを加えてもう一度混ぜ、塩、こしょうで味を調える。

Potato salad

4-5 potatoes(450g)
1 cucumber
1/2 small onion
2 ham slices
5-6 tbsp mayonnaise
salt and pepper

1. Peel and cut each potato into 4-6 pieces. Soak them in water and drain. Line a microwave-resistant bowl with some paper towel and add the potatoes. Cover loosely with plastic wrap and microwave for 5-6 minutes until tender.

2. Remove the plastic wrap and paper towel from the bowl. Mash the potatoes while they are hot and let it cool.

* To boil in a pot, follow these instructions: Thoroughly wash unpeeled whole potatoes, put them in a pot, cover with water, put on a lid and turn on the heat. When it comes to a boil, turn the heat down to low, and cook for 20-25 minutes until tender. Peel the skin and put them in a bowl while they are still hot and mash them.

3. Thinly slice the cucumber. Toss with a little salt and let it stand for 5 minutes. When it starts to soften, squeeze the excessive moisture out.

4. Thinly slice the onion, soak in water for 5 minutes, and squeeze.

5. Cut the slices of ham in half and then cut into 1cm-wide strips.

6. Add the cucumber, onion, and ham to the mashed potatoes, and mix together. Add the mayonnaise and mix again. Season with salt and pepper to taste.

ほうれんそうの
ピーナツあえ

Spinach
with peanut sauce

ほうれんそうとピーナツバターは
どこの国でも手に入るので、海
外に行くとよくつくります。簡単
なレシピですが、ほうれんそう
のゆで加減と水けをしっかり絞
ることがおいしくつくるコツです。

This dish is made with spinach and peanut butter, both of
which are readily available in
any country. Therefore, I often
cook this when I am overseas.
It is a very simple and easy
recipe. Be sure not to overcook
the spinach and to thoroughly
squeeze the excess water out.
This is necessary to make the
dish excellent.

ほうれんそうのピーナツあえ

【 材料 4人分 】

ほうれんそう　200g

ピーナツバター
　（加糖タイプ）　大さじ3

砂糖　小さじ1

しょうゆ　小さじ1

みりん　小さじ2

塩　適宜

ピーナツ　適宜

1. ボウルにピーナツバター、砂糖、しょうゆ、みりんを入れ、よく混ぜ合わせる。

2. ほうれんそうは5cm長さに切って茎と葉に分ける。塩少々を入れた熱湯で茎、葉の順にサッとゆでる。冷水にとり、ざるに上げて水けをよくきり、水けを絞る。

3. 1に2を加えてあえる。味をみて足りなければ塩少々で調える。

4. 器にほうれんそうを盛り、粗く切ったピーナツを上からかける。

Spinach with peanut sauce

【 Serves 4 】

200g spinach

3 tbsp peanut butter
　(sweetened type)

1 tsp sugar

1 tsp soy sauce

2 tsp mirin

salt

peanuts

1. Mix the peanut butter, sugar, soy sauce, and mirin in a bowl.

2. Cut the spinach into 5cm-long pieces and separate the leaves from the stems. Blanch the stems first in boiling water with a pinch of salt, and then add the leaves. Plunge in cold water and then drain well. Squeeze out the excess water.

3. Add the spinach to the peanut sauce and mix. Check the taste and add a little salt if necessary.

4. Serve the spinach onto a plate and sprinkle coarsely chopped peanuts on top.

トマトのおひたし

Tomato *ohitashi*

おひたしというと青菜でつくることが多
いですが、わたしはいろいろな食材で
つくっています。オクラ、きのこ、すりお
ろした山芋でつくったりもします。どん
な野菜を入れてもいいので、皆さんの国
にあるもので自由につくってみてください。

Ohitashi is often made with leafy vegetables, but I make it with all kinds of
ingredients, such as okra, mushroom,
grated yam, among others. This recipe
works for any vegetable, so please feel
free to be creative with whatever ingredient comes in handy in your country.

トマトのおひたし

ミディトマト　2パック（400g）
だし　カップ1+1/2（300ml）
みりん　大さじ2
うす口しょうゆ　大さじ2

1. 容器にだし、みりん、うす口しょうゆを合わせる。

2. トマトはヘタを取り、先端に浅く切り込みを入れる。

3. 沸騰した湯にトマトを入れ、すぐに冷水にとり、水けをきって皮をむく。

4. 1にトマトを浸し、ラップをして冷蔵庫に入れて冷やし、味をなじませる。

Tomato *ohitashi*

2 packs middle-sized
  tomatoes(400g)

1+1/2cups(300ml) dashi

2 tbsp mirin

2 tbsp light soy sauce

1. Combine dashi, mirin and light soy sauce in a container.

2. Remove the stems of the tomatoes. Slice a shallow cut into the bottom of the tomatoes.

3. Place the tomatoes into boiling water. Put them into a bowl of cold water immediately, drain them, and peel off the skins.

4. Soak the tomatoes in the dashi mixture prepared in step 1. Cover the container with plastic wrap. Chill in the refrigerator to let the tomatoes absorb the flavors.

コールスローサラダ

Coleslaw

酸味があって少し甘めのコールスローが好きです。水っぽくなるとおいしくないので、ドレッシングを混ぜる前にキャベツとにんじんの水けをしっかりと絞ることがポイントです。

I like coleslaw that is sour and a bit sweet. It wouldn't taste good if it gets watery, so the key is to thoroughly squeeze the excess water from the shredded cabbage and carrot before mixing in the dressing.

コールスローサラダ

【 材料 つくりやすい分量 】

キャベツ　4〜5枚（400g）
にんじん　50g
塩　小さじ1+1/2

[調味料]
マヨネーズ　大さじ6
酢　大さじ3
砂糖　小さじ1

塩・こしょう　各少々

1. キャベツは1cm角に切ってボウルに入れる。
2. にんじんは皮をむき、8mm角の薄切りにしてボウルに加える。分量の塩を入れて混ぜ、10〜15分おく。水けが出たらさらしなどで水けをよく絞る。
3. 調味料を混ぜ合わせておく。
4. キャベツとにんじんのボウルに調味料を加えて混ぜ、味をみて塩、こしょうで調える。

Coleslaw

4-5 leaves cabbage(400g)
50g carrot
1+1/2 tsp salt

[dressing]
6 tbsp mayonnaise
3 tbsp vinegar
1 tsp sugar

salt, pepper

1. Cut the cabbage into 1cm squares and put them into a bowl.
2. Peel the carrot, thinly slice it into 8mm squares and add them into the bowl. Mix in the salt, and leave for 10-15 minutes. When excess water comes out, squeeze it out thoroughly using a cheesecloth, etc.
3. Combine the ingredients for the dressing in a bowl.
4. Add the mixture of dressing to the bowl of cabbage and carrot, and mix well. Season with salt and pepper.

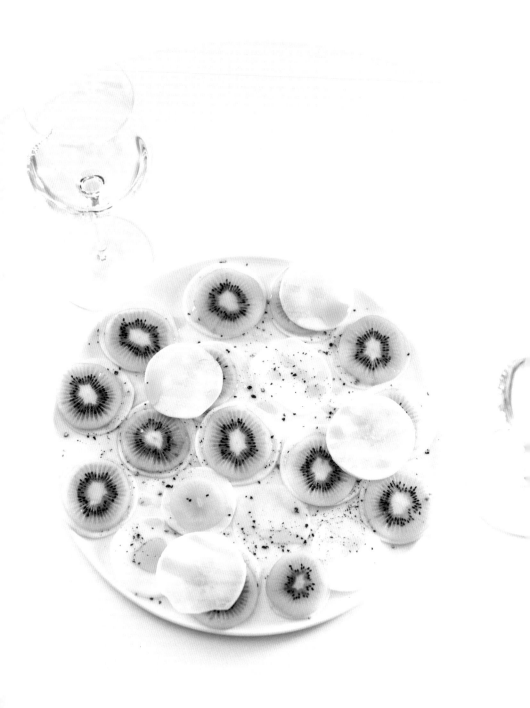

かぶとキウイの
カルパッチョ

Turnip and kiwifruit
carpaccio

材料を切り、冷蔵庫でしっかりと冷やして
おけば、あとは盛りつけるだけ。5分もあれ
ばできてしまう料理です。簡単なレシピを
いくつか持っておくと人を招いたときなど
に便利。わたしは最後の盛りつけを友人た
ちの前でやって喜ばれています。

All you have to do is to cut the ingredients
and chill them well in the fridge. All that
is left is to arrange them on a plate. This
simple dish is ready in just 5 minutes.
Having several easy recipes like this one
will come in handy when you have people
over. I entertain my friends by arranging
the food on the plate in front of them.

かぶとキウイのカルパッチョ

【 材料 4人分 】

かぶ　2〜3コ
キウイ　1〜2コ
塩・こしょう　各少々
オリーブ油　適宜

1. かぶは茎を落として皮をむき、横に薄い輪切りにする。
2. キウイは皮をむいて薄い輪切りにする。
3. 器にかぶをのせて塩、こしょうをふり、キウイを上に重ね、ところどころにかぶを重ねて食べる直前まで冷蔵庫で冷やしておく。
4. 食べる際にオリーブ油を回しかける。

Turnip and kiwifruit carpaccio

2-3 turnips

1-2 kiwifruits

salt, pepper

olive oil

1. Cut the stems off the turnips, peel, and cut into thin round slices.
2. Peel the kiwifruits and cut them into thin round slices.
3. Place the turnip slices on a serving plate, sprinkle some salt and pepper. Place the kiwifruit slices on top of the layer of turnip. Add some turnip slices on top of the kiwifruit partially, and let it cool in the refrigerator until serving.
4. Sprinkle olive oil right before eating.

たたききゅうりの
酢じょうゆ漬け

Easy pickled cucumber

箸休めとしての小さなおかずです。たくさんごちそうがあっても、結局わが家でいちばんおいしいと言われるのがこのレシピ。つくったその日だけでなく、2日目、3日目と味がだんだんしみたところもおいしいので、たくさんつくって楽しんでください。

This is a small side dish. But this dish is always the most popular among my family even when there are other delicacies on the table. This is good not just on the day it is made, but it gets tastier in the next few days as it absorbs more flavor. So make plenty at a time and enjoy !

たたききゅうりの酢じょうゆ漬け

きゅうり　6本

しょうが　1かけ

しょうゆ　カップ1/2（100ml）

酢　カップ1/2（100ml）

砂糖　大さじ4

赤とうがらし（小口切り）
　　1～2本分

1. しょうゆ、酢、砂糖を混ぜ合わせる。

2. きゅうりは両端を切り落とし、すりこ木や麺棒で割れ目ができる程度にたたく。1本を4～6等分に切る。

3. しょうがはせん切りにする。

4. きゅうりをポリ袋に入れ、1の漬け汁、赤とうがらしを加える。冷蔵庫で2～3時間以上おく。

5. 食べる直前にしょうがのせん切りを入れて味をなじませる。

Easy pickled cucumber

6 cucumbers

1 knob ginger

1/2 cup(100ml) soy sauce

1/2 cup(100ml) vinegar

4 tbsp sugar

1-2 red chili peppers,
    chopped

1. Combine the soy sauce, vinegar, and sugar.

2. Trim the ends of the cucumbers and strike them with a rolling pin to make cracks. Cut each cucumber into 4-6 pieces.

3. Cut the ginger into fine strips.

4. Put the cucumbers into a plastic bag and add the mixture prepared in step 1 and the red chili pepper. Let stand in the refrigerator for at least 2-3 hours.

5. Add the ginger strips right before serving to let the cucumbers absorb the flavor.

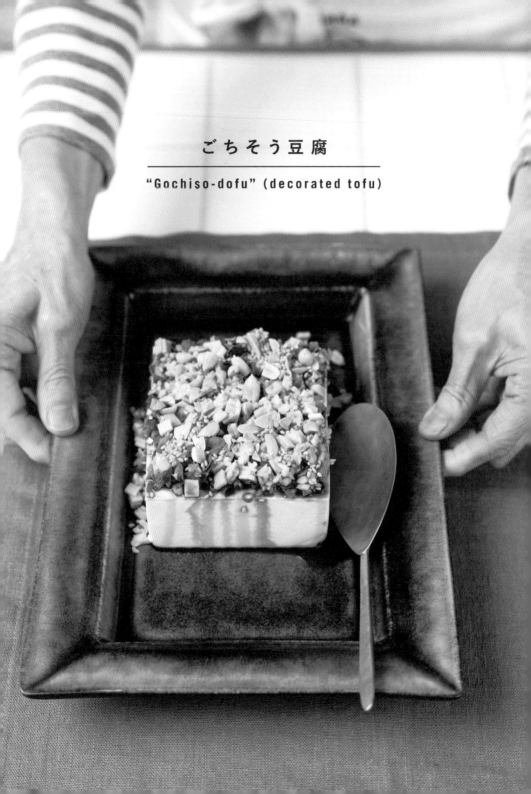

ごちそう豆腐

"Gochiso-dofu" (decorated tofu)

食感の違うもの、味の違うものなどを、とにかく細かく切ってのせたごちそう豆腐。トッピングは、いつも冷蔵庫の残り物で考えています。急なお客様のときに便利な一品としてわたしの定番です。きれいな盛りつけをするために、豆腐より2cm高く紙タオルで回りを巻いて、豆腐の水けを吸わせたり、トッピングが落ちないように工夫したり、万能しょうゆは上からかけず、豆腐のふちに沿って少しずつかけたり、ちょっとしたことが大切です。

This *gochiso-dofu* is served with all kinds of ingredients cut into small pieces that have different textures or tastes. Toppings on tofu are usually leftovers from my fridge. This is a very convenient and smart dish when we have unexpected guests at our home.

To keep the pleasant appearance of the toppings, it is important to pay attention to details such as wrapping the paper towel around the tofu to absorb excess water, making the edge of the towel extend 2cm above the tofu so the toppings don't fall off, and pouring the sauce little by little along the edge of the tofu.

ごちそう豆腐

【 材料 2〜4人分 】

絹ごし豆腐　1丁

ハム　2枚
（ローストビーフ、ローストチキン、
ツナなどでも代用可）

しょうが　20g

細ねぎ（小口切り）　大さじ3

青じそ　5枚

ピーナツ・白ごま　各適宜

［万能しょうゆ］

昆布（5cm角）　1枚

みりん　カップ1/4（50ml）

しょうゆ　カップ3/4（150ml）

1. 万能しょうゆをつくる。昆布は軽く洗って紙タオルでふく。小鍋にみりんを入れて煮立て、1〜2分煮詰め、火を止める。熱いうちにしょうゆと昆布を加え、1時間以上おいて昆布を取り出す。

2. 豆腐は水けをきって器に盛る。紙タオルを豆腐より2cm高くなるように巻き、余分な水けを吸わせる。冷蔵庫に入れ、十分に冷やしておく。

3. トッピングのハム、しょうが、細ねぎ、青じそ、ピーナツは刻む。

4. 冷やした豆腐の上に3のトッピングをのせてからごまをふり、紙タオルを取り除く。

5. 盛りつけをくずさないよう、万能しょうゆは上からかけずにふちに沿って少しずつかける。

"Gochiso-dofu" (decorated tofu)

[Serves 2~4]

1 pack soft tofu

2 slices ham
(Roast beef, roast chicken,
or canned tuna
can be substituted.)

20g ginger

3 tbsp chopped spring onion

5 shiso leaves (green perilla)

peanuts, white sesame seeds
--- to taste

[all-purpose soy sauce]

1 piece kombu kelp
(5cm square)

1/4 cup(50ml) mirin

3/4 cup(150ml) soy sauce

1. Make the all-purpose soy sauce:
    Rinse the kombu lightly, and wipe
    with a paper towel. Put the mirin
    in a small pan and bring to a boil.
    Boil it for 1-2 minutes, and turn
    off the heat. Add the soy sauce
    and kombu while still hot. Let it
    stand for more than 1 hour and
    then remove the kombu.

2. Drain the tofu and place on a
    serving plate. Wrap a folded
    paper towel around the sides of
    the tofu to absorb excess water.
    Make sure the edge of the paper
    towel extends 2cm above the
    tofu. Place in the refrigerator to
    chill the tofu thoroughly.

3. Chop up the toppings: ham, ginger,
    spring onion, shiso, and peanuts.

4. Pile the toppings from step 3 on
    the chilled tofu. Sprinkle sesame
    seeds, and remove the paper towel.

5. Pour the all-purpose soy sauce
    little by little along the edge of
    the tofu so that it doesn't disturb
    the beautifully arranged toppings.

豆腐ラザニア

Tofu lasagna

ラザニアといえばパスタですが、わが家は
豆腐やなすを使います。手間がかかってい
るように見えますが、ホワイトソースの代わ
りに生クリームを使うので手軽につくれま
す。チーズはたっぷりとのせてくださいね。

Lasagna is originally made of pasta.
However, I use tofu or eggplant instead.
You may think making lasagna is time-
consuming, but with my recipe, you can
easily cook it using heavy cream instead
of white sauce. Please put plenty of
cheese on top.

豆腐ラザニア

絹ごし豆腐　2丁

ミートソース
　（下記参照
　　または市販）
　　カップ2（400ml）

生クリーム
　　カップ1/4（50ml）

ピザ用チーズ　150g

オリーブ油　大さじ2

塩・こしょう　各少々

1. 豆腐は紙タオルで包み、15分ほどおいて水けをきり、1丁を5枚に切る。
2. フライパンにオリーブ油を入れ、中火にかける。豆腐を並べ、塩、こしょうをふり、両面をこんがりと焼く。
3. オーブンは230℃に温めておく。
4. 耐熱皿の底にミートソースを薄く敷き、豆腐をその上に並べ、生クリームを注ぐ。これをくり返し、チーズを散らす。
5. オーブンで15〜20分焼く。

ミートソース

合いびき肉　500g

ベーコン　50g

玉ねぎ　1コ（200g）

にんじん　小1/2本（50g）

セロリ　1/2本（50g）

マッシュルーム　1パック（100g）

にんにく（みじん切り）　1かけ分

オリーブ油　大さじ2

塩・こしょう　各少々

赤ワイン　カップ1/2（100ml）

ドミグラスソース（市販）1缶（290g）

トマトジュース　カップ1（200ml）

[A]

ウスターソース　大さじ1

トマトケチャップ　大さじ2

塩・こしょう　各少々

1. ベーコンはみじん切りにする。
2. 玉ねぎ、にんじん、セロリは3〜4mmの角切りにする。
3. マッシュルームは4〜5等分にスライスする。
4. フライパンにオリーブ油を熱し、にんにく、ベーコンを炒め、ひき肉を加えて炒め、軽く塩、こしょうをふる。玉ねぎ、にんじん、セロリを加えて混ぜ、マッシュルームも炒める。
5. 赤ワインを加え、ひと煮立ちさせてドミグラスソースとトマトジュースを加える。弱火で約20〜25分煮て、Aで味を調える。

Tofu lasagna

[Serves 4]

2 packs soft tofu

2 cups (400ml)
  meat sauce
  (see the recipe below
  or use store-bought)

1/4 cup (50ml)
  heavy cream

150g pizza cheese

2 tbsp olive oil

salt and pepper

1. Wrap the tofu in a paper towel for about 15 minutes to drain. Then, cut each piece into five slices.
2. Put the olive oil in a frying pan and turn the heat on medium. Place the tofu in the frying pan and season with salt and pepper. Brown the tofu slowly on both sides.
3. Preheat the oven to 230°C.
4. Spread a thin layer of meat sauce on the bottom of a baking dish. Place the tofu on top. Pour the cream over the layer of tofu. Repeat this process, and sprinkle the cheese on top.
5. Bake in the oven for 15-20 minutes.

Meat sauce

[Serves 4]

500g ground meat (mixed beef and pork)

50g bacon

1 onion (200g)

1/2 small carrot (50g)

1/2 stalk celery (50g)

1 pack mushrooms (100g)

1 clove garlic (finely chopped)

2 tbsp olive oil

salt, pepper

1/2 cup (100ml) red wine

1 can (290g)
  demi-glace sauce (store-bought)

1 cup (200ml) tomato juice

[A]

1 tbsp Worcester sauce

2 tbsp tomato ketchup

salt, pepper

1. Finely chop the bacon.
2. Cut the onion, carrot, and celery into 3-4mm squares.
3. Slice each mushroom into 4-5 pieces.
4. Heat the olive oil in a frying pan and stir-fry the garlic and bacon. Add the ground meat and stir-fry. Lightly sprinkle salt and pepper. Add the onion, carrot and celery and stir. Add the mushrooms and stir-fry.
5. Pour in the red wine and let it come to a boil. Add the demi-glace sauce and tomato juice, and let it simmer over low heat for 20-25 minutes. Season with [A].

いんげんと豚ひき肉の
香味炒め

Stir-fried string beans
and ground pork

夫が大好きでよくつくる料理です。野菜
は、さやいんげんのほかに、なすやピー
マン、絹さやなどでもおいしくできます。
いんげんだけ食べてしまってひき肉が残っ
てしまうことがあるのですが、そんなとき
はご飯の上にかけたり、ラーメンやチャー
ハンに入れるとおいしく食べられます。

I often cook this dish because my husband loves it. Instead of using string
beans, you can also cook it with eggplant, green pepper, or snow peas.
Sometimes I end up with only the meat
left on the plate after I have eaten up
the beans. But, in that case, it is a good
idea to put the meat on top of the white
rice or to use it for extra flavor when
you cook *ramen* noodles or fried rice.

いんげんと豚ひき肉の香味炒め

【 材料 4人分 】

さやいんげん　400g

豚ひき肉　150g

長ねぎ（みじん切り）　1/2本分

しょうが（みじん切り）　大さじ2

にんにく（みじん切り）　大さじ1

サラダ油　大さじ1

紹興酒または酒　大さじ1

しょうゆ　大さじ4

赤とうがらし（小口切り）　1〜2本分

ごま油　大さじ1

1. さやいんげんは筋を取ってゆでる。流水にとって冷まし、水けを取って食べやすい大きさの斜め切りにする。

2. フライパンにサラダ油を熱し、長ねぎ、しょうが、にんにくを炒める。香りがたったら豚ひき肉を加えて炒める。

3. 肉に火が通ったら紹興酒、さやいんげんを加えて炒める。しょうゆ、赤とうがらしを加えて全体に混ぜ合わせる。仕上げにごま油を回しかける。

Stir-fried string beans and ground pork

[Serves 4]

400g string beans

150g ground pork

1/2 finely chopped
Japanese leek

2 tbsp finely
chopped ginger

1 tbsp finely
chopped garlic

1 tbsp vegetable oil

1 tbsp *shokoshu*
(Chinese sake)
or Japanese sake

4 tbsp soy sauce

1-2 red chili peppers,
chopped

1 tbsp sesame oil

1. Remove the strings of the beans and boil. Chill under cold running water. Pat dry and cut diagonally into bite-sized pieces.

2. Heat the oil in a frying pan. Add the leek, ginger, and garlic, and stir-fry. When you can smell the aroma of the leek, ginger, and garlic, add the ground pork and stir-fry.

3. When the pork is cooked, add the *shokoshu* and string beans, and continue to stir-fry. Add the soy sauce and red peppers and mix thoroughly. Finish by drizzling the sesame oil over it.

甘辛粉吹きいも

"Kofuki-imo" (salty-sweet flavored potatoes)

イギリスで初めてこの料理をつくったとき、イギリス人の友達にとても驚かれたのを覚えています。じゃがいもをしょうゆと砂糖で甘辛く煮たものは想像がつかなかったよう。でも食べてみるとおいしいと、大好評。最後に加えるバターが、味の決め手です。

When I first served this dish to my British friends in the U.K., I remember everyone was very surprised. This potato recipe, cooked with soy sauce and sugar, was totally unfamiliar to them. But once they ate it, they all loved it. A scoop of butter that I add before serving it is the key. It gives a rich flavor to the taste.

甘辛粉吹きいも

じゃがいも　4コ（600g）
砂糖　大さじ3
しょうゆ　大さじ2
バター　20g

1. ボウルなどに砂糖としょうゆを合わせ、砂糖が溶けるまでよく混ぜる。

2. じゃがいもは皮をむいて四つ割りにする。鍋に入れ、じゃがいもがかぶるまで水を加えて火にかける。煮立ったらふたをして弱火にし、10〜15分、柔らかくなるまでゆでる。

3. じゃがいものゆで汁をよくきり、再び火にかけて水分をとばす。1を加え、手早くからめながら混ぜ、最後にバターを入れて全体にからめて火を止める。

"Kofuki-imo"
(salty-sweet flavored potatoes)

[Serves 4]

---

4 potatoes (600g)

3 tbsp sugar

2 tbsp soy sauce

20g butter

1. Combine the sugar and soy sauce in a bowl, and mix well until the sugar dissolves.

2. Peel the potatoes and cut them into quarters. Put the potatoes in a pan, cover with water, and turn on the heat. When it comes to a boil, put a lid on, turn down the heat and simmer for 10-15 minutes in low heat until tender.

3. Drain the potatoes well, put it over the heat again and cook off the moisture. Add the sauce from step 1, and stir briskly while coating the potatoes with the sauce. Add the butter at the end and toss the potatoes, and turn off the heat.

もう30年以上前からつくっている料理で、夫の大
好物です。グラタンといってもホワイトソースではな
く、生クリームをかけて焼くだけ。じゃがいもは、あ
らかじめ電子レンジで十分に柔らかくしておくこと
がポイントです。むずかしそうに見えて、実はとても
簡単なので気軽につくってみてください。

I have been cooking this gratin for over 30 years
now and this is one of my husband's favorites.
Instead of white sauce, I simply pour heavy cream
over the ingredients and bake it in the oven. The
important point is to put the potatoes in the microwave beforehand, until they are tender. It may
look difficult, but in fact this dish is very easy.
Please try it for yourself.

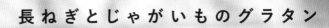
長ねぎとじゃがいものグラタン

Japanese leek and potato gratin

長ねぎとじゃがいものグラタン

【 材料 4人分 】

じゃがいも　3コ（400g）
長ねぎ　2本
アンチョビ　2〜3枚
ピザ用チーズ　150〜200g
生クリーム　カップ1（200ml）
塩・こしょう　各適宜

1. オーブンは220〜230℃に温めておく。
2. じゃがいもは皮をむいて5〜6mm厚さの輪切りまたは半月切りにする。水にさらし、水けをよくきる。
3. 耐熱皿に紙タオルを数枚敷き、じゃがいもを均等にのせる。ラップでふんわりと覆い、電子レンジ（600W）に6〜8分、柔らかくなるまでかける。ラップと紙タオルを取り除く。
4. アンチョビは手で小さくちぎる。長ねぎは4〜5cm長さに切り、縦に薄切りにする。
5. アンチョビと長ねぎをじゃがいもの間にはさむ。
6. 生クリームを塩、こしょうで味つけし、じゃがいもにまんべんなくかける。チーズを散らし、オーブンで20〜25分ほど焼く。

Japanese leek and potato gratin

[Serves 4]

3 potatoes (400g)

2 Japanese leeks

2-3 anchovy fillets

150-200g pizza cheese

1 cup(200ml) heavy cream

salt and pepper --- to taste

1. Preheat the oven to 220-230°C.

2. Peel the potatoes and slice them into 5-6mm-thick rounds (*wagiri*) *or* half-moons (*hangetsu-giri*). Soak in water and drain well.

3. Place a few pieces of paper towel on a heat-resistant dish. Put the potatoes on it evenly. Cover with plastic wrap loosely. Microwave for 6-8 minutes until soft. Remove the plastic wrap and paper towel.

4. Tear the anchovies into small pieces. Cut the Japanese leeks into 4-5cm-long pieces, and thinly slice lengthwise.

5. Put the anchovies and the Japanese leeks between the layers of potatoes.

6. Season the heavy cream with salt and pepper and pour over the potatoes evenly. Sprinkle with cheese on top and bake in the oven for 20-25 minutes.

野菜の揚げびたし

Deep-fried vegetables in *mentsuyu*

わたしはいろいろなたれをつくって楽しんでいます。中でもめんつゆは、麺料理だけでなく、煮物に、丼にと便利に使い回しています。今回は、つくりおきができる野菜の揚げびたしをご紹介します。レシピにある野菜のほかにも、れんこん、ごぼう、いも類などでもおいしくできます。

I enjoy making various kinds of sauces in my kitchen, but "mentsuyu" especially comes in handy because it can be used not only for noodles but also for many recipes such as simmered dishes or "donburi" (a bowl of rice topped with meat or vegetable and sauce). In this book, I will show you how to make deep-fried vegetables in *mentsuyu* that can be kept in the refrigerator. For this recipe, you can use lotus root, burdock root, or various kinds of potatoes.

野 菜 の 揚 げ び た し

なす　3コ

かぼちゃ　1/8コ

グリーンアスパラガス　4本

パプリカ（赤）　1/2コ

パプリカ（黄）　1/2コ

さやいんげん　50g

めんつゆ　カップ2（400ml）
　（225ページ参照）

揚げ油　適宜

1. なすはヘタを取り除き、縦半分に切ってから4等分にする。5分ほど水にさらして水けをふき取る。

2. かぼちゃは種を取り除き、1.5cm厚さの食べやすい大きさに切る。耐熱皿に紙タオルを敷いてかぼちゃをのせ、電子レンジ（600W）に1～2分かける。

3. アスパラガスは根元の堅い部分を切り落とし、はかまを取り、斜め4等分に切る。

4. パプリカは縦半分に切って種を取り、長さを半分に切って細切りにする。

5. さやいんげんは筋を取り、斜め半分に切る。

6. めんつゆはバットなど、浅い容器に入れておく。

7. 野菜を油で揚げ、油をきる。熱いうちにめんつゆにつける。

8. 温かいままでも、冷やして食べてもよい。冷蔵庫で2～3日保存できる。

Deep-fried vegetables in *mentsuyu*

[Serves 4]

3 eggplants

1/8 pumpkin
(*kabocha* squash)

4 spears green asparagus

1/2 red pepper

1/2 yellow pepper

50g string beans

2 cups(400ml) *mentsuyu*
(see page 225)

vegetable oil
--- for deep-frying

1. Remove the stems of the eggplants and cut them in half lengthwise. Then cut them into 4 pieces. Soak the eggplants in water for about 5 minutes and pat dry.

2. Remove the seeds of the pumpkin and cut into 1.5cm-thick, bite-sized pieces. Place a paper towel on a heat-resistant plate, put the pumpkin pieces on top, and microwave at 600W for 1-2 minutes.

3. Cut off the woody part of the asparagus and remove the scales. Cut each asparagus into 4 pieces diagonally.

4. Cut each pepper in half lengthwise and remove the seeds. Cut in half crosswise and slice into thin strips.

5. String the beans, and cut them diagonally in half.

6. Put the *mentsuyu* in a shallow dish.

7. Deep-fry all the vegetables in oil and drain them. Soak them in *mentsuyu* while still hot.

8. Serve hot or cold. You can keep the vegetables in the refrigerator for 2-3 days.

お弁当 | Bento (box lunch)

お弁当

小さな箱の中にご飯や色とりどりのおかずを詰めた日本のお弁当。

ふたをあけるときのわくわく感が楽しいと、

海外でも bento としてすっかりその人気が定着しています。

わたしのお弁当づくりは子どもが幼稚園のときから

高校を卒業するまでの約14年間、続いていました。

振り返ると、お弁当づくりから学ぶことがたくさんあったなと思います。

「どう入れたらおいしく食べてもらえるだろう、喜んでくれるだろう」

ということを思いながら、色合いや味のバランス、

盛りつけなど毎日工夫を重ねていく。

朝の忙しい限られた時間の中で、

段取りよく進めるために常備菜を活用したり、

夕食づくりのついでに下ごしらえをしたり、

お弁当を丁寧につくっているうちに料理が上手になることに気がつきました。

お弁当づくりにルールはありません。

この本で紹介した料理で好きなものがあったら

それを詰めてみることから始めてください。

お弁当箱に詰めてみるとまた違ったおいしさが感じられると思います。

Bento (box lunch)

The Japanese bento, or box lunches are tightly packed
with colorful foods and rice.
It has fascinated many people overseas, who find it fun
and exciting to open the bento box, and the name "bento"
has become widely acknowledged throughout the world.
I started making bento for my children
when they entered kindergarten and continued
for 14 years till they graduated from high school.
Looking back, I realize that I learned a lot through bento-making.
"What's the best way to pack it?",
"How can I make one that they would love?"
I was constantly thinking these thoughts,
and was trying different methods on a daily basis to make a bento
that had a good balance in taste and color,
and looked appealing to the eye.
Because mornings are always busy, I have developed time-saving
and efficient techniques such as packing into the bento box side dishes
that are usually kept in the fridge for days,
or doing the preparation for bento
while making dinner the night before.
I realized that all these years of putting a lot of effort into
making bento has made me better at cooking.
There are no ground rules in bento-making.
If you find a recipe you like in this book,
please start by putting that into the bento.
You will find that it will have a different appeal
once packed in a bento.

日本の料理道具
Japanese cooking utensils

【 巻きす 】
Makisu

【 盤台・しゃもじ 】
Handai　Shamoji

【 おろし金 】
Oroshigane

【 ごまいり 】
Goma-iri

【 菜箸・盛りつけ箸 】
Saibashi Moritsuke-bashi

【 土鍋 】
Donabe

【 蒸し器 】
Mushiki

日本の料理道具

Japanese cooking utensils

日本料理にはたくさんの道具があります。どれも日本の手仕事の技で丁寧につくられていて、使えば使うほど理にかなったものだなと実感します。日本中の手仕事をしている皆さんに感謝しながら使わなければいけないと思っています。

There are many different kinds of utensils for Japanese cooking. Each is made with great attention to detail by the hands of Japanese artisans, and the more I use them, the more I am impressed with how practical they are. Every time I use the tools, I feel a sense of appreciation towards all the craftsmen throughout Japan.

【盤台・しゃもじ】

Handai (wooden sushi tub, wide cooking bowl)
Shamoji (rice paddle)

すし飯をつくるときに使う道具。余分な水分を吸ってくれるので、すし飯がおいしくできます。

Tools used for making sushi rice. They absorb the excess water and help make delicious sushi rice.

【巻きす】　*Makisu* (rolling mat)

主に巻きずしをつくるときに使う道具で、竹でできています。卵焼きの形を整えたり、ゆでた野菜の水けを絞るときなどにも使います。

Mainly used for making sushi rolls. Made of bamboo. It can also be used to arrange the shape of the *tamago-yaki* (rolled Japanese omelet), squeeze out excess water from boiled vegetables, etc.

【おろし金】　*Oroshigane* (grater)

日本にはいろいろなタイプのおろし金があります。左は鬼おろしといって粗い大根おろしをつくるための道具。粗くおろすことで水分が出ず、ふんわりとしたおいしい大根おろしになります。中央のおろし金は銅製で、職人の手仕事でつくられています。右はわさびをするための専用の道具。サメの皮でできています。これを使うと空気を含んでなめらかなおろしわさびになります。

There are various types of graters in Japan. The one on the left is called *Oni-oroshi*, and it is used for coarsely grating daikon. By coarsely grating, loss of moisture is kept at a minimum, making for a fluffy, tasty daikon-oroshi. The one in the center is made of copper, crafted by the hands of an artisan. The one on the right is made from shark skin, and is exclusively used for grating wasabi. By using this, you can make airy and creamy grated wasabi.

【ごまいり】

Goma-iri (sesame seed toaster)

ごまをいるための専用の道具。フライパンでもできますが、これを使うと焦げずに上手にいることができ、香ばしい風味が増します。

A utensil specifically for toasting sesame seeds. You can substitute it with a frying pan, but this tool will allow you to toast sesame seeds without burning them, and will enhance the fragrance.

【菜箸・盛りつけ箸】

Saibashi Moritsuke-bashi
(cooking chopsticks and serving chopsticks)

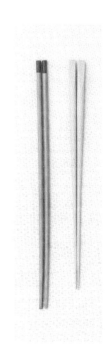

食事のための箸ではなく、調理に使う箸です。菜箸は炒め物をはじめ、料理全般に使います。盛りつけ箸は盛りつけ専用の箸で、先端は細くとがっていて、細かいものまでつまめるようになっています。反対側は斜めになっていて、柔らかいものをつぶさずにはさんだり、へらのように使ったりします。

These chopsticks are not for eating a meal, but for cooking or serving a meal. *Saibashi* is used for stir-frying and for cooking in general. *Moritsuke-bashi* is used exclusively for serving. The narrow end has a sharp, pointy edge, enabling it to pick up even the smallest items. The opposite end is slanted, so it can be used like a spatula, or to pick up soft items without squashing.

【土鍋】　*Donabe* (Japanese clay pot)

陶製の鍋です。鍋料理に使われることが多いですが、保温性が高く、ご飯やおかゆを炊いたり、煮込み料理にと幅広く使っています。

This is a ceramic pot. It is often used for making hot pot dishes but because of its excellent heat retention ability, it is quite versatile and I use it for cooking rice and simmering dishes, and so on.

【蒸し器】　*Mushiki* (steamer)

和食には蒸す料理も多くあり、蒸し器は大切な調理道具のひとつです。特に茶碗蒸しは海外の人に人気です。蒸し器でつくると料理はやさしい味になって野菜はおいしさを感じます。

Many Japanese dishes involve steaming in the process, so the steamer is an important cooking tool. *Chawan-mushi* savory custard is especially popular among people overseas. The steamer enhances the flavor of vegetables, and gives dishes a mild taste.

すり鉢
Mortar

すり鉢は小さいものから大きなものまでたくさんあります。母がごま料理をよくつくっていたので、小さいときからすり鉢でごまをする手伝いをよくしていました。このすり鉢は母が使っていたものです。長い間使っていたのでひびもありますが、これからも受け継いで使っていこうと思っています。

市販の練りごまもありますが、すり鉢で自分ですってみるとおいしさに驚きます。大切に使って、いつか子どもたちが使ってくれたときにわたしを思い出してくれるといいなと思います。

Mortars vary in size, from small to large. My mother used to make dishes with sesame seeds quite often. So to help her out, I have been grinding sesame seeds in a mortar since I was little. This mortar is the one my mother used. It has been in use for such a long time that is has cracks in it, but I intend to continue using this mortar, passed down from my mother.

There are ready-made sesame pastes available in stores, but nothing compares to the one you make with your own hands using a mortar. I intend to use this mortar with care, and pass it on to my children. I hope it will remind them of me when they use it someday.

3

RICE, NOODLES
& MORE

ご飯もの、麺、
その他

牛 丼

Gyudon
(beef on rice)

牛丼は日本では人気のファストフードの一つ。具は玉ねぎと牛肉だけ、とシンプルなので海外でもつくりやすい料理です。白ワインで煮ることで牛肉が柔らかくなるので、堅い部位のもので十分おいしくできます。

Gyudon is one of the most popular fast foods in Japan. The main ingredients are only onion and beef, so making this outside of Japan is easy. Even inexpensive, tough beef can be delicious because simmering with white wine softens the beef.

牛 丼

【 材料 4人分 】

牛薄切り肉　500g
玉ねぎ　4コ（800g）
白ワイン　カップ2（400ml）
水　カップ1（200ml）
しょうゆ　カップ3/4（150ml）
みりん　カップ1/2（100ml）
砂糖　大さじ4
ご飯　適宜
紅しょうが　適宜

1. 玉ねぎは1cm厚さの半月切りにする。
2. 牛肉は6〜7cm長さに切る。
3. 水と白ワインを合わせて中火にかけ、煮立ったら牛肉を加える。アクを取り、弱火にして10〜15分ほど煮る。牛肉が堅い場合は少し長く煮る。
4. しょうゆ、みりん、砂糖を加えて落としぶたをし、約10分煮る。
5. 玉ねぎを加え、玉ねぎが透き通ったら火を止め、そのままおいて味をなじませる。
6. 温かいご飯の上に汁ごとのせ、紅しょうがを添える。

Gyudon (beef on rice)

500g thinly sliced beef
4 onions (800g)
2 cups (400ml) white wine
1 cup (200ml) water
3/4 cup (150ml) soy sauce
1/2 cup (100ml) mirin
4 tbsp sugar
cooked rice
red pickled ginger to taste

1. Slice the onions into 1cm-thick *hangetsu-giri* pieces (see page 280).
2. Cut the beef into 6-7cm lengths.
3. Heat the water and white wine on medium heat. When it comes to a boil, add the beef. Skim the surface of the broth. Turn the heat to low and simmer it for 10-15 minutes. If the beef is still hard, simmer it a little longer.
4. Add the soy sauce, mirin, and sugar, and cover it with a drop-lid. Simmer for about 10 minutes.
5. Add the onions, and simmer until translucent. Turn off the heat and let it stand.
6. Serve this along with the sauce on top of hot cooked rice. Garnish with a little red pickled ginger.

親子丼

Chicken and egg on rice

時々、無性に食べたくなる料理がだれにでもあると思いますが、わたしは親子丼がその一つです。急に食べたくなっても、いつも鶏肉を冷凍しているのでつくることができます。卵のとろりとした食感が大事なので、卵を加えたら火を止めてふたをし、余熱で半熟状態にしてください。

Have you ever experienced a sudden intense craving for a certain dish? For me, *oyako-don* is one such dish. This recipe is easy. So, whenever I feel like eating *oyako-don*, I can prepare it right away because I always have some chicken in my freezer.

To keep the smooth and soft texture of egg, which is very important, turn off the heat after adding the egg and put a lid on the pan to half-cook the egg with residual heat.

親 子 丼

鶏もも肉（皮つき）
　　小1枚（200g）
玉ねぎ　1/2コ
卵　4コ
ご飯　適宜
みつば（刻む）　適宜

[合わせ調味料]
だし　カップ1/2（100ml）
しょうゆ　大さじ3
砂糖　大さじ2
みりん　大さじ2

のり・漬物　各適宜

1. 玉ねぎは6〜7mm幅の薄切りにする。鶏肉は小さめの一口大に切る。

2. 合わせ調味料を混ぜる。

3. 卵は2コずつ溶き卵にしておく。

4. 鍋に2の半量を煮立てる。鶏肉の半量を加えて少し煮てから、玉ねぎの半量を加えて1〜2分煮る。

5. 煮立っているうちに、2コ分の溶き卵の2/3量を流し入れる。ふたをして半熟状くらいに煮えたら鍋のふちから残りの溶き卵を流し入れる。火を止め、みつばを入れてふたをして蒸らす。（やや半熟状態になるくらいがよい）もう1人分も同様にしてつくる。

6. 丼にご飯を盛り、具をのせる。もみのり、漬物を添える。

Chicken and egg on rice

[Serves 2]

1 boneless small chicken
   thigh with skin(200g)

1/2 onion

4 eggs

cooked rice

mitsuba (trefoil), chopped
   --- for garnish

[dashi mixture]

1/2 cup (100ml) dashi

3 tbsp soy sauce

2 tbsp sugar

2 tbsp mirin

nori seaweed, pickles
   --- for garnish

1. Slice the onion into 6-7mm-thick pieces. Cut the chicken into smaller bite-sized pieces.

2. Combine the ingredients for the dashi mixture.

3. Beat 2 eggs in 2 separate bowls.

4. Put half of the dashi mixture into a pan and bring to a boil. Add half of the chicken and cook for a short time. Add half of the onion slices and simmer for 1-2 minutes.

5. While it is simmering, pour two-thirds of the 2 beaten eggs and put on a lid. When it is half-cooked, pour the remaining one-third of the beaten eggs evenly around the rim of the pan. Turn off the heat, add the *mitsuba*, and allow to settle with the lid on.
   (The egg should be slightly runny.)
   Repeat the process to make another serving.

6. Divide the rice in individual bowls and put the chicken and egg on top. Garnish with some nori and pickles.

しょうがご飯

Ginger rice

しょうがは米と一緒に炊き込まず、炊き上がってから加えて混ぜるので、しょうががしっかりと香ります。おにぎりにして、パリパリののりと一緒によく食べます。

The ginger is added after the rice is cooked, not cooked with it. By doing this, the aroma of the ginger is stronger. I often eat this dish with crisp nori seaweed.

しょうがご飯

米　カップ2（400ml）
しょうが　30g
油揚げ　2枚
うす口しょうゆ　大さじ2
みりん　大さじ1
酒　大さじ1
だし　適宜
塩　少々

1．米は洗ってざるに上げ、10〜15分おく。

2．しょうがはみじん切りにする。

3．油揚げは油抜きしてから水けを軽く絞り、ふき取る。5mm角に切る。

4．うす口しょうゆ、みりん、酒を合わせ、だしを足してカップ2（400ml）に計量する。

5．厚手の鍋に米を入れ、油揚げをのせ、調味しただしを入れる。

6．ふたをして火にかけ、沸騰したら弱火にして10〜12分ほど炊く。火を止め、約10分そのままおいて蒸らし、しょうがを加えてサックリと混ぜる。味をみて足りなければ塩少々で味を調える。

Ginger rice

2 cups (400ml) rice

30g ginger

2 pieces *abura-age*
(thinly sliced deep-fried tofu)

2 tbsp light soy sauce

1 tbsp mirin

1 tbsp sake

dashi

salt

1. Wash the rice well and drain. Let it stand for 10-15 minutes.
2. Mince the ginger finely.
3. Pour hot water over the *abura-age* to remove excess oil, squeeze lightly, and pat dry. Cut it into 5mm square pieces.
4. Combine the light soy sauce, mirin, and sake, and add enough dashi to make 400ml of sauce.
5. Put the rice in a heavy pan. Add the *abura-age* and dashi mixture.
6. Cover and place over high heat. When it comes to a boil, turn down the heat and cook for 10-12 minutes. Turn off the heat, and let it stand for about 10 minutes to allow settling. Then mix in the ginger. Season to taste with a little salt if necessary.

豚肉と野菜の
炊き込みご飯

Steamed rice with pork
and vegetables

やさしい味の炊き込みご飯も好きです
が、これは濃いめの味です。あらかじめ
肉に調味料をしっかり含ませ、その肉か
ら出るうまみでご飯を炊きます。肉のほ
かに大豆も入るので、ボリューム満点です。

Sometimes I like a light taste for *takiko-mi gohan* (rice steamed with vegetables, meat, or fish). However, the one I introduce here has a rich flavor. The meat should be deeply dressed with seasoning beforehand so that its "umami" (soup from the seasoned meat) can soak well into the rice during the cooking process. As it uses soybeans as well as meat, this recipe is hearty.

豚肉と野菜の炊き込みご飯

【 材料 4人分 】

米　カップ2（400ml）
豚薄切り肉　150g

［豚肉の下味］
しょうゆ　大さじ2
砂糖　大さじ1/2
しょうが汁　小さじ1

にんじん　1/2本
生しいたけ　2〜3枚
ゆで大豆　カップ1（200ml）
しょうゆ　大さじ1
みりん　大さじ1
酒　大さじ1
だし　適宜
塩　少々

1. 米は洗ってざるに上げ、10〜15分おく。

2. 豚肉はこま切れにし、しょうゆ、砂糖、しょうが汁で下味をつける。

3. にんじんは皮をむいて小さめのいちょう切りにする。しいたけは軸を落とし、2cm角に切る。

4. 鍋に米を入れ、にんじん、しいたけ、ゆで大豆を散らし、豚肉を重ならないようにのせる。

5. しょうゆとみりん、酒を計量カップに注ぎ、だしを加えて400mlにする。塩で味を調え、鍋のふちから静かに注ぎ入れる。ふたをし、強火にかける。煮立ったら弱火にし、10〜12分、炊く。

6. 炊き上がったら火を止め、10分ほどそのままおいてよく混ぜ合わせる。

Steamed rice with pork and vegetables

[Serves 4]

2 cups (400ml) rice

150g sliced pork

[marinade sauce for pork]

2 tbsp soy sauce

1/2 tbsp sugar

1 tsp juice
from grated ginger

1/2 carrot

2-3 fresh shiitake
mushrooms

1 cup(200ml)
boiled soybeans

1 tbsp soy sauce

1 tbsp mirin

1 tbsp sake

dashi

salt

1. Wash the rice and drain in a strainer. Let it stand for 10-15 minutes.

2. Chop the pork into tiny pieces and marinate in soy sauce, sugar, and juice from grated ginger.

3. Peel the carrot and cut into small *icho-giri* pieces(see page 280). Cut off the stems of the shiitake mushrooms and cut into 2cm squares.

4. Put the rice in a pan and scatter the carrot, shiitake mushrooms, and soybeans. Top it with the marinated pork, making sure they don't overlap.

5. Pour the soy sauce, mirin, and sake into a measuring cup. Add the dashi until it measures 400ml and season with salt. Gently pour the dashi mixture onto the rice from the rim of the pan. Put a lid on and turn the heat on high. When it comes to a boil, turn the heat down to low and cook for 10-12 minutes.

6. When the rice is cooked, turn off the heat and let it stand for about 10 minutes. Stir the rice well.

三色丼
Three-color rice bowl

どこの家庭でもつくられる、日本の家庭
料理の一つです。これは母から習ったも
ので、そぼろのひき肉を一度下煮し、そ
の煮汁でご飯を炊きます。
少し手間はかかりますが、その分おいしく、
わたしもこのやり方が気に入ってつくって
います。卵を細かくいることと、絹さやを細
く切ってたくさんのせるのがおいしいです。

This is one of the Japanese home-
cooked dishes which is served in typical
Japanese families. Here, I introduce the
recipe that my mother taught me. After
quickly simmering ground meat in a
pan, use the original broth from boiling
the meat to cook the rice.
This takes time and effort, but it adds
richness to the taste and I like it this
way. I believe the important point here
is to scramble the eggs finely and to use
plenty of thinly sliced snow peas on top
of white rice.

三 色 丼

【 材料 4人分 】

米　カップ2（400ml）
　　（洗ってざるに上げておく。
　　14ページ参照）
鶏ひき肉　300g
絹さや　100g
だし　適宜
塩　少々
のり　適宜
紅しょうが　適宜

［A］
しょうゆ　大さじ1
酒　大さじ1
みりん　大さじ1

［B］
しょうゆ　大さじ2+1/2〜3
酒　大さじ1
みりん　大さじ2
砂糖　大さじ1+1/2〜2

［いり卵］
卵　4コ
砂糖　大さじ1+1/2〜2
酒　大さじ2
塩　少々

1. 鍋にだしカップ1（200ml）と［A］の材料を合わせて煮立て、鶏ひき肉を加えて煮る。鶏肉に火が通ったらこして煮汁とひき肉を分けておく。
2. 計量カップに煮汁を入れ、だしを加えて400mlにする。塩少々で味を調える。
3. 炊飯器に米を入れ、だしと合わせた煮汁を加えて炊く。
   * 炊飯器でなく、鍋で炊く場合は、14ページのご飯の炊き方を参照。
4. 別の鍋に［B］の材料を合わせて煮立て、1の鶏ひき肉を加えてほとんど汁けがなくなるまで煮る。
5. いり卵をつくる。ボウルに卵を溶きほぐし、砂糖、酒、塩を加えて混ぜ合わせる。鍋に流し入れ、中火にかける。卵のふちが固まりかけたら弱火にし、4本の菜箸でかき混ぜながら火を通す。
6. 絹さやはサッとゆでて冷水にとり、水けをきって斜め細切りにする。
7. 丼にご飯を盛り、鶏そぼろ、いり卵、絹さやを盛りつける。もみのりを散らし、紅しょうがを添える。

Three-color rice bowl

[Serves 4]

2 cups (400ml) rice,
   washed and drained
   (see page 15)
300g ground chicken
100g snow peas
dashi
salt
nori seaweed
   --- for garnish
red pickled ginger
   --- for garnish

[A]
1 tbsp soy sauce
1 tbsp sake
1 tbsp mirin

[B]
2+1/2 - 3 tbsp soy sauce
1 tbsp sake
2 tbsp mirin
1+1/2 - 2 tbsp sugar

[scrambled eggs]
4 eggs
1+1/2 - 2 tbsp sugar
2 tbsp sake
salt --- a little

1. Combine 1 cup/200ml dashi and the ingredients of [A] in a pan and bring to a boil. Add the ground chicken and simmer. When the chicken is cooked, strain it to separate the soup and chicken.

2. Put the soup into a measuring cup and add more dashi until it measures 400ml. Season with a little salt.

3. Put the rice in a rice cooker and add the dashi mixture. Turn on the rice cooker.

   * If you want to use a pan instead of a rice cooker, see page 15.

4. Combine the ingredients of [B] in another pan and bring to a boil. Add the cooked chicken and simmer until the sauce is almost gone.

5. Make scrambled eggs : Beat the eggs in a bowl. Add the sugar, sake, and salt, and mix together. Pour the egg in a pan and turn the heat on medium. When the rim of the egg has just set, turn the heat down to low and stir the mixture with 4 chopsticks until it is cooked.

6. Blanch the snow peas and chill in cold water. Drain and cut diagonally into thin strips.

7. Divide the rice into individual bowls. Arrange the chicken, eggs, and snow peas on top. Garnish with some nori and red pickled ginger.

カツ丼

"Katsu-don"
(pork cutlet on rice)

わたしは、卵は半熟くらいがおいしいので、好きです。この片手の小さな鍋は、わたしが生まれる前から使っている、カツ丼や親子丼をつくる専用の道具です。ちょうど丼1杯分の量がつくれる大きさで、鍋から直接ご飯に具をのせられる形になっています。

I like my eggs half-cooked for *katsu-don*. This small skillet with a handle is made specifically for cooking *katsu-don* or *oyako-don*. My mother used this before I was born, and I use it to this day. It's a good size for cooking just enough for one *donburi* bowl, and is designed to make it easy to directly pour the contents of the pan over rice.

カ ツ 丼

豚カツ　1枚

玉ねぎ　1/4コ

卵　2コ

だし　カップ1/2（100ml）

砂糖　大さじ1

しょうゆ　大さじ2

みりん　大さじ1

ご飯　適宜

1．豚カツは食べやすい大きさに切る。

2．玉ねぎは薄切りにする。

3．卵は溶いておく。

4．だし、砂糖、しょうゆ、みりんを浅い鍋に入れ、中火で温める。玉ねぎを加えて少し煮、豚カツを加えてしばらく煮る。煮立ったら溶き卵を回しかけ、ふたをして1分ほど加熱して火を止める。

5．丼にご飯を盛り、4をのせる。

"Katsu-don" (pork cutlet on rice)

[Serves 1]

1 *tonkatsu*

1/4 onion

2 eggs

1/2 cup(100ml) dashi

1 tbsp sugar

2 tbsp soy sauce

1 tbsp mirin

cooked rice

1. Cut the cutlet into bite-sized pieces.
2. Slice the onion thinly.
3. Beat the eggs.
4. Combine the dashi, sugar, soy sauce, and mirin in a shallow pan. Warm it on medium heat and add the onion. Simmer for a short time, add the cutlet, and continue cooking for a while. When it comes to a boil, pour the beaten egg over the cutlet and cover with a lid for 1 minute before turning the heat off.
5. Put the rice in a serving bowl and place the cooked cutlet on top.

レンジ赤飯

Microwaved "sekihan"
(azuki beans and rice)

日本ではお祝い事にはつきもののお赤飯ですが、夫もわたしも大好きなのでふだんからよくつくっています。本来は蒸し器でつくるものですが、ちょっと食べたいときに気軽につくれるようにと、電子レンジでできるこのレシピを考えました。

Sekihan is usually served on celebratory occasions in Japan. But I often cook it regardless of occasion as my husband and I both love it. Traditionally, it is cooked in a steamer, but I came up with this idea to use a microwave to cook it easily whenever I feel like eating *sekihan*.

＊お使いの機種によっては仕上がりが多少柔らかくなることがあります。記載された加熱時間を目安に適宜調整してください。

＊The *sekihan* might become a little bit too soft depending on the microwave type. Please adjust the cooking time as needed by using the times given here as a reference.

レンジ赤飯

もち米　カップ2（400ml）
小豆　60g
いりごま（黒）　適宜
塩　適宜

1. 小豆はたっぷりの水に2〜3時間つけておく。
2. もち米は洗って30分ほど水につけ、水けをきる。
3. 鍋に小豆と水300mlを入れ、弱火にかける。小豆を堅めにゆでる。
   * 指でつぶせるくらい柔らかいものはゆですぎ。堅めにゆで上げること。
4. 小豆をざるに上げ、ゆで汁はとっておく。ゆで汁に水を足して300mlにし、冷ましておく。
5. 耐熱ボウルに小豆、もち米、ゆで汁を入れ、ふんわりとラップで覆う。電子レンジ（600W）に約9分かける。
6. 電子レンジから取り出し、混ぜ合わせる。再びラップをし、もう2〜3分かける。
7. 茶碗に盛り、ごま塩をふる。

Microwaved "sekihan" (azuki beans and rice)

[Serves 4]

2 cups(400ml)
  mochigome (glutinous rice)
60g dry azuki beans
roasted black sesame seeds
  --- to serve
salt --- to serve

1. Soak the azuki beans in plenty of water for 2-3 hours.
2. Wash the glutinous rice. Soak in water for about 30 minutes and drain.
3. Put the azuki beans in a pan and add 300ml water. Place the pan over low heat and simmer until the beans are barely cooked.
   * If the beans can be crushed with fingers, they are overcooked. Make sure some firmness remains.
4. Drain the azuki beans in a strainer, saving the water they were cooked in. Add more water until it measures 300ml. Set aside and cool.
5. Put the azuki beans, rice, and the water in a heat-resistant bowl. Cover it loosely with plastic wrap and microwave on 600W for about 9 minutes.
6. Remove from the microwave and stir well. Cover the bowl with plastic wrap once again and microwave for 2-3 more minutes.
7. Serve in a serving bowl and sprinkle with sesame seeds and salt to taste.

一年を通していろいろなおすしをつくりますが、ひな祭りの季節には、ちらしずしが欠かせません。具はここで紹介したものがすべてそろわなくても大丈夫ですが、錦糸卵のつくり方は覚えてみてください。細く切って空気を含ませるようにふんわりとほぐすだけで、とても華やかになります。最初は薄く焼けなくても大丈夫。練習すれば上手になります。

I cook various kinds of sushi throughout the year. But in the *Hina-matsuri* (Doll Festival) season in early March, I never fail to make "chirashi-zushi." If you don't have all the ingredients I introduced here, don't worry about it. But please learn how to make *kinshi-tamago* (shredded egg crepes). Thinly shred the egg crepes, loosen the shreds, and put them on top of the sushi in a fluffy manner. This makes the dish look very gorgeous. Don't worry if at first you cannot make the egg crepes thinly. With practice you will get the knack.

ちらしずし

"Chirashi-zushi"

ちらしずし

[すし飯]
米　カップ2（400ml）
水　カップ2（400ml）

[すし酢]
酢　カップ1/2（100ml）
砂糖　大さじ1+1/2〜2
塩　小さじ1

[干ししいたけの甘煮]
干ししいたけ　8枚
だし　カップ1/2（100ml）
砂糖　大さじ2
しょうゆ　大さじ1+1/2
酒　大さじ1
みりん　大さじ1

[酢れんこん]
れんこん　1節（200g）
酢　大さじ5
砂糖　大さじ2
塩　少々

1. すし酢をつくる。ボウルに酢、砂糖、塩を入れ、よく混ぜて溶かす。

2. すし飯をつくる。米は洗ってざるに上げ、約15分おいて水けをきり、鍋に入れて同量の水を加えて炊く。炊きたてのご飯にすし酢を加え、切るように混ぜて粗熱を取る。

3. 干ししいたけの甘煮を煮る。干ししいたけは少なめの水で十分に戻す。水けを軽く絞り、石づきを取る。鍋にだしと調味料を合わせて煮立て、しいたけを入れ、落としぶたをして弱火で10〜15分、煮汁が少なくなるまで煮て火を止め、そのままおいて味を含ませる。冷めたら4等分に切る。

4. 酢れんこんをつくる。れんこんは皮をむき、1cm厚さのいちょう切りにして水にさらし、水けをよくふく。鍋に調味料を合わせて煮立て、れんこんを加えて中火で手早く混ぜながら1〜2分煮て火を止め、粗熱を取る。

"Chirashi-zushi"

[Serves 4]

[sushi rice]
2 cups(400ml) rice
2 cups(400ml) water

[sushi vinegar]
1/2 cup (100ml)
   vinegar
1+1/2〜2 tbsp sugar
1 tsp salt

[sweet simmered
   shiitake muhrooms]
8 dried shiitake
   mushrooms
1/2 cup (100ml)
   dashi
2 tbsp sugar
1+1/2 tbsp soy sauce
1 tbsp sake
1 tbsp mirin

[vinegared lotus root]
1 lotus root (200g)
5 tbsp vinegar
2 tbsp sugar
salt

1. Make sushi vinegar: Combine the vinegar, sugar, salt in a bowl, mix well and dissolve.

2. Make sushi rice: Wash the rice and drain it in a strainer. Let it stand for about 15 minutes. Put the rice in a pan, add the same amount of water to the pan as rice and cook. Pour sushi vinegar over freshly cooked rice and fold it in while cooling the rice.

3. Make sweet simmered shiitake mushrooms: Soak the dried shiitake mushrooms in water until they become soft. Lightly squeeze them to drain and cut off the stems. Combine the dashi with other ingredients in a pot and bring to a boil. Add the shiitake mushrooms, cover with a drop-lid and simmer over low heat for 10-15 minutes until the liquid is reduced. Turn off the heat and let it stand for a while to let the mushrooms absorb the sauce. When cooled, cut into quarters.

4. Make vinegared lotus root: Peel and cut the lotus root into 1cm-thick *icho-giri* (quarter-rounds) pieces. Soak in water and drain well. Combine the seasonings in a pan and bring to a boil. Add the lotus root and simmer for 1-2 minutes over middle heat while stirring quickly. Let it cool.

ちらしずし

［錦糸卵］
卵　2コ
砂糖　大さじ1
酒　大さじ1/2
塩　少々

サラダ油　適宜

［刺身］
まぐろ（赤身）　1サク
白身魚（たいなど）　1サク
ゆでだこの足　1本

すだち・しょうがの甘酢漬け・
　もみのり　各適宜
しょうゆ・おろしわさび　各適宜

5. 錦糸卵をつくる。ボウルに卵を溶きほぐし、調味料を加えてよく混ぜ、ざるでこす。小さめのフライパンにサラダ油を熱し、紙タオルでならす。卵液を少量流し入れて薄く広げ、焼き色がつく前に裏返して両面を焼き、薄焼き卵をつくる。残りの卵液も同様に焼く。薄焼き卵を重ねて軽く巻き、細いせん切りにして空気を入れるようにふんわりとほぐす。

6. 刺身はそれぞれ食べやすく1.5 ～2cm角に切る。

7. 器にすし飯を盛り、錦糸卵をたっぷりとのせる。刺身、干ししいたけの甘煮、酢れんこんを散らす。すだち、好みでしょうがの甘酢漬けを添え、もみのりをのせる。刺身にはわさび、しょうゆをつけていただく。

"Chirashi-zushi"

[kinshi-tamago
(shredded egg crepe)]

2 eggs

1 tbsp sugar

1/2 tbsp sake

salt

vegetable oil

[sashimi]

1 saku block
tuna (lean)

1 saku block
white-flesh fish
(sea bream etc.)

1 leg boiled octopus

sudachi, pickled
ginger, crumbled
nori seaweed
--- for garnish

soy sauce,
grated wasabi
--- for sashimi

5. Make kinshi-tamago (shredded egg crepes): Beat the eggs in a bowl, add the sugar, sake and salt, mix well and strain. Using a paper towel, grease a small frying pan with some vegetable oil. Pour a small amount of egg mixture in the pan, and spread it out to make a thin layer. Before the surface of the egg turns color, flip it over and cook the other side as well. Remove the egg crepe from the pan. Repeat the same processs with the rest of the egg mixture. Stack up the egg crepes, roll them together and cut them into thin strips. Loosen them gently by pulling them apart to let some air in.

6. Cut the sashimi into 1.5-2cm cubes.

7. Serve the sushi rice onto a plate, top it with plenty of kinshi-tamago. Scatter diced sashimi, sweet simmered shiitake mushrooms, and vinegared lotus root on top. Garnish with sudachi, pickled ginger to taste. Top it with crumbled nori seaweed. Serve with wasabi and soy sauce for the sashimi.

裏巻きずし
_____

"Uramaki-zushi"
(inside-out sushi rolls)

海外に行っていちばん多くつくっている一品。アボカド、青じそ、マヨネーズ、かにかまぼこ、の順に具をのせて巻くと色がきれいで上手につくれます。この組み合わせがどこでも手に入る材料で、この組み合わせはだれでも好きな味です。

I often make this dish when I am overseas. The trick is to be sure to add the filling in the correct order: first the avocado, then the shiso leaves, mayonnaise, and crab sticks. This way you will make an excellent roll and the color will be beautiful. These fillings are available anywhere, and are everyone's favorites.

裏 巻 き ず し

[すし飯]
米　カップ2(400ml)
水　カップ2(400ml)
米酢　カップ1/2(100ml)
砂糖　大さじ1+1/2〜2
塩　小さじ1

かにかまぼこ　18本
アボカド　1〜1+1/2コ
青じそ　9枚
焼きのり　3枚
マヨネーズ　適宜
いりごま(白)　適宜

1. 194ページの要領ですし飯をつくる。
2. のりは半分に切る。オーブン用の紙は、のりより一回り大きく切る。
3. アボカドは種と皮を取り、1コを12等分のくし形に切る。青じそは半分に切る。
4. 巻きすにオーブン用の紙をのせ、のりをのせる。すし飯を薄く広げ、のりが上になるように裏返す。
5. 中心より少し手前にアボカドを1列に並べる。青じそをのせ、マヨネーズを小さじ1程度ぬり、かにかまぼこをのせる。
6. 具を一巻きして軽く押さえ、オーブン用の紙を巻き込まないように、端まで巻く。巻き終わりを下にしてもう一度軽く押さえ、巻きすとオーブン用の紙を外す。
7. 表面にごまをまんべんなくつけ、6等分に切り分ける。

"Uramaki-zushi" (inside-out sushi rolls)

[Makes 6 rolls]

[sushi rice]

2 cups (400ml) rice

2 cups (400ml) water

1/2 cup (100ml) rice vinegar

1+1/2-2 tbsp sugar

1 tsp salt

18 crab sticks

1-1+1/2 avocado

9 shiso leaves
  (green perilla)

3 sheets toasted
  nori seaweed

mayonnaise --- to taste

toasted white sesame seeds
  for coating

1. Make sushi rice according to the instructions on page 195.

2. Cut the nori seaweed in half. Cut the parchment paper into squares that are slightly larger than the nori.

3. Peel and stone the avocado. Cut each one into 12 equal pieces (wedges). Cut the shiso leaves in half.

4. Place the parchment paper onto a *makisu* (rolling mat). Place the nori on top and spread a layer of sushi rice on it. Turn the nori over, so that the nori side faces upwards.

5. A little below the halfway point, make a thin line of avocado strips. Place the shiso leaves on top and spread 1 tsp of mayonnaise thinly over them. Then place the crab sticks on top.

6. Roll the *makisu* up and over the ingredients, pressing it gently. Continue rolling to the edge, making sure you don't roll up the paper in the sushi. Press lightly again, sealed side down, and remove the *makisu* and the paper.

7. Coat the sushi rolls with sesame seeds. Cut each roll into 6 pieces.

ビーフカレー

Beef curry

カレーは日本の人気家庭料理のベスト3に入る料理です。市販のカレールーを使ってつくるのが一般的ですが、これはスパイスを使って丁寧につくるレシピ。玉ねぎの甘みと肉のうまみが味の決め手なので、玉ねぎはしっかりと炒めて甘さを引き出してください。

Curried rice is one of the three most popular dishes in Japanese home-cooked meals. It is common to make it with store-bought curry paste, but this recipe takes a more elaborate approach and uses various spices. The sweetness of the onions and the flavor of the meat determine this dish, so make sure to stir-fry the onions thoroughly to pull out their natural sweetness.

ビーフカレー

牛肩ロース肉（塊）　1kg

塩　小さじ1

こしょう　少々

小麦粉　大さじ3

玉ねぎ　4コ（1kg）

にんじん　2本（300g）

じゃがいも　4コ

トマト　2コ（400g）

クミンシード　小さじ1

おろしにんにく　大さじ1

おろししょうが　大さじ1

カレー粉　大さじ3

［スパイス］

ガラムマサラ・ターメリック・
　コリアンダーなどのパウダー
　各少々

カルダモン（すりつぶす）　5粒分

水　カップ6（1200ml）

サラダ油　適宜

塩・こしょう　各少々

トマトケチャップ　大さじ3

ウスターソース　大さじ1
　（または、とんかつソース）

ご飯　適宜

福神漬　適宜

1. 玉ねぎは薄切りにする。

2. にんじんは皮をむいて2cm厚さの輪切り、または半月切りにする。

3. じゃがいもは皮をむいて4等分にし、水にさらして水けをよくきる。

4. 牛肉は3～4cm角に切る。

5. 鍋にサラダ油大さじ2を弱火で熱し、クミンシードを入れて炒める。香りが出たら玉ねぎを加えて強めの中火で炒め、水分をとばしてから弱火であめ色になるまで炒める。にんにく、しょうがを加えて炒める。カレー粉、スパイスを加え、粉っぽさがなくなり香りがよくなったら水を加えてのばす。

6. 牛肉に分量の塩とこしょうをふってよくすり込み、小麦粉をまぶす。

7. 別のフライパンにサラダ油大さじ2を熱し、牛肉を焼きつける。全面に焼き色がついたら5の鍋に入れ、煮立ったらアクを取り、ふたをして30～40分煮る。

8. 牛肉が柔らかくなったらザク切りにしたトマトを入れ、トマトが柔らかくなったらにんじん、じゃがいもを加えてさらに10～15分煮る。火が通ったら、塩、こしょう、ケチャップ、ソースで味を調える。

9. 器にご飯を盛り、ビーフカレーをかけ、好みで福神漬を添える。

Beef curry

1kg beef shoulder loin
   (block)

1 tsp salt

pepper

3 tbsp flour

4 onions (1kg)

2 carrots (300g)

4 potatoes

2 tomatoes (400g)

1 tsp cumin seeds

1 tbsp grated garlic

1 tbsp grated ginger

3 tbsp curry powder

[powdered spices]

garam masala,
   turmeric,
   coriander etc.
   --- a bit of each

5 cardamom seeds
   (ground)

6 cups(1200ml) water

vegetable oil

salt, pepper

3 tbsp tomato ketchup

1 tbsp Worcester sauce
   (or *tonkatsu* sauce)

cooked rice

fukujinzuke pickles
   --- to serve

1. Thinly slice the onions.

2. Peel the carrots and slice into 2cm-thick rounds or half-moons.

3. Peel the potatoes and cut them into quarters. Soak them into water, and drain well.

4. Cut the beef into 3-4cm cubes.

5. Heat 2 tbsp of vegetable oil in a pan over low heat, and stir-fry the cumin seeds until fragrant. Add the onion and stir-fry over medium high heat to cook off the moisture, then lower the heat and continue to stir-fry until golden brown. Add the garlic and ginger and stir-fry. Add the curry powder and other spices and stir-fry until they mix well and become fragrant. Add the water and dilute.

6. Sprinkle 1 tsp of salt and a small amount of pepper on the beef and rub them in. Then, coat it with flour.

7. Heat 2 tbsp of vegetable oil in a separate frying pan, and sear the beef. When browned, add it into the pan in step 5. When it comes to a boil, skim the surface, put on a lid, and let it simmer for 30-40 minutes.

8. When the beef is tender, add the coarsely cut tomatoes and cook until they are soft. Add the carrots and potatoes and simmer for another 10-15 minutes. When cooked through, season with some salt, pepper, ketchup and Worcester sauce.

9. Put some rice in a serving bowl and pour some beef curry on top. Garnish with *fukujinzuke* pickles to taste.

なすのドライカレー

Curried rice with eggplant

なすのドライカレーは、子どもが小さい
ころからよくつくっているレシピです。な
すを揚げると甘みが出ておいしくなりま
す。つけ合わせの酢じょうゆ卵は、これ
だけを食べてもおいしいので、ぜひつ
くってみてください。冷蔵庫で一晩つけ
ると味がよくしみておいしくなります。

Curried rice with eggplant has been
my favorite recipe since my children
were little. The natural sweetness of
the eggplant comes out when it is fried.
The pickled eggs, for the side dish,
taste good by themselves, so please
try them. The eggs will taste delicious
after being marinated overnight in the
fridge, as they will soak in the flavors.

なすのドライカレー

【 材料 4人分 】

合いびき肉　400g

なす　4〜6コ

玉ねぎ　1コ

ピーマン　2コ

カレー粉　大さじ2

カレールー（市販。刻んだもの）　大さじ2

スパイス（ガラムマサラ・
　ターメリック・クミン・コリアンダー
　などのパウダー）　各少々

トマトケチャップ　大さじ1

とんかつソース　大さじ1

揚げ油　適宜

サラダ油　大さじ2

塩・こしょう　各適宜

酢じょうゆ卵　適宜

玄米など好みのご飯・
福神漬　各適宜

1. 玉ねぎは1cm角に切る。

2. ピーマンは縦半分に切って種を取り、
　1cm角に切る。

3. なすはヘタを落として3cm厚さの輪切
　りにする。水にさらし、水けをきってふく。
　鍋に揚げ油を熱し、なすを揚げて中まで
　火を通し、油をよくきる。

4. 深めのフライパンにサラダ油を熱し、合
　いびき肉を炒める。肉の色が変わったら
　玉ねぎを加えて炒め合わせる。

6. カレー粉、カレールー、スパイス、トマト
　ケチャップ、とんかつソースを加えて混ぜ、
　ピーマンを加え混ぜる。火を止め、塩、こ
　しょうで味を調え、揚げたなすを加える。

6. 温かいご飯にカレーをかけ、酢じょうゆ
　卵、福神漬を添える。

酢じょうゆ卵

【 材料 4人分 】

卵　6〜8コ

しょうゆ　大さじ2

酢　大さじ1

砂糖　小さじ1

1. 鍋に卵を入れ、卵がかぶるまで水を入れて火にか
　け、沸騰したら弱めの中火にし、水から約12分ゆ
　でる。冷水にとって殻をむき、水けをふき取る。

2. ポリ袋などに調味料を入れて混ぜ合わせ、卵をつける。

3. 空気を抜いて口を閉じ、冷蔵庫で2〜3時間おくと
　食べられる。

Curried rice with eggplant

[Serves 4]

400g ground beef and pork
  mixture

4-6 eggplants

1 onion

2 green peppers

2 tbsp curry powder

2 tbsp curry paste
  (store-bought, chopped)

powdered spices
  (garam masala, turmeric,
  cumin, coriander, etc.)
  --- a bit of each

1 tbsp tomato ketchup

1 tbsp *tonkatsu* sauce

vegetable oil for deep-frying

2 tbsp vegetable oil

salt, pepper

pickled egg

preferred cooked rice
  (ex. brown rice)

fukujinzuke pickles --- to serve

1. Cut the onions into 1cm squares.
2. Cut the green peppers in half and remove the seeds. Then chop them into 1cm-square pieces.
3. Trim the eggplants and cut into 3cm-thick round slices. Soak them in water. Drain and pat dry. Heat the deep-frying oil in the frying pan, and deep-fry the eggplants until cooked through. Drain well.
4. Heat the vegetable oil in another deep-frying pan. Add the ground meat and stir-fry. When the meat is browned, add the onions and continue to stir-fry.
5. Add the curry powder, curry paste, spices, tomato ketchup, and *tonkatsu* sauce, and mix. Mix in the green peppers and turn off the heat. Season with salt and pepper, and add the fried eggplants.
6. Ladle the warm curry over warm rice and add the pickled egg and *fukujinzuke*.

Pickled eggs

[Serves 4]

6-8 eggs

2 tbsp soy sauce

1 tbsp vinegar

1 tsp sugar

1. Place the eggs in a pot, cover them with cold water, and heat the pot. When it comes to a boil, turn down the heat to medium low. Let it boil for about 12 minutes from cold water. Then, put the eggs in cold water, peel them, and wipe off excess water.
2. Combine the seasonings in a plastic bag, and soak the eggs in the marinade.
3. Drain the air from the plastic bag, seal it, and let the eggs marinate in the refrigerator for 2-3 hours before eating.

大切にしたい日本の手仕事　漆（うるし）

A Japanese handicraft
that should be cherished
urushi lacquerware

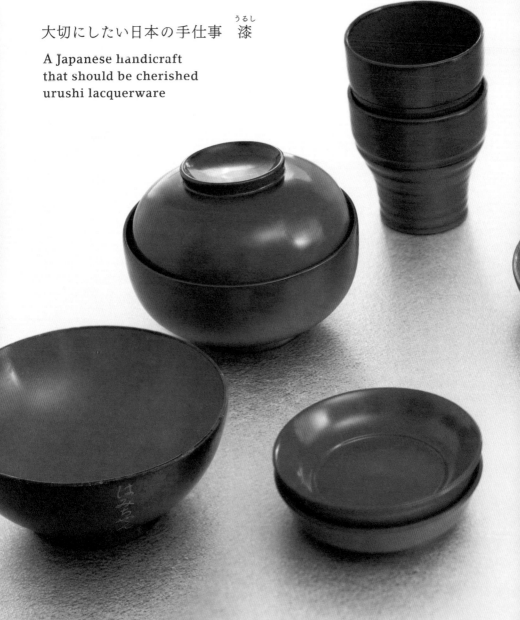

漆

お椀にお箸、重箱、茶たく、酒器。日本にはさまざまな漆器があります。漆は古くからある日本の伝統工芸で、日本を象徴するものでもあります。漆の器は、お正月など特別なときに使うという印象があるようですが、わたしの実家では、母が漆好きなので、みそ汁のお椀やお弁当箱などいろいろな漆器が身近にありました。物心ついたときから使っていた名前入りの漆の汁椀は、今でも大切に持っています。漆のすばらしさに触れるにつれ、漆が大好きになり、作家さんの仕事場を訪ねたり、自分でデザインしたり…。今ではたくさんの漆の器が集まりました。

漆はデリケートなので、傷をつけないようやさしく洗い、しっかりと水けをふいて乾かしてからしまうなど、扱いにちょっとした気遣いが必要ですが、きちんと手入れをすれば一生使うことができます。また、その美しさもさることながら、料理が冷めにくく温まりにくいなど、機能的にも優れています。若い世代の人たちにはあまり使われなくなってきていますが、漆に限らず、日本の伝統工芸や手仕事のものがわたしたちの生活からなくなっていくのは本当にさびしいことです。

いい道具は、暮らしを楽しく、豊かにしてくれます。少しずつでも、漆のよさが見直され、これからも人々の暮らしの中に浸透していってほしい。そのためにも日本のすぐれた技術を、大切に次世代へ伝えていかないといけないと思っています。

漆のお弁当箱。お弁当箱としてだけでなく、ばらしてペアの器としても使えます。

Urushi lacquer lunchbox. It can be used as a lunch-box or, when separated, a pair of serving dishes.

Urushi

In Japan, there are various shikki (lacquerware goods) such as owan (wooden bowls), chopsticks, jubako (multi-tiered boxes), chataku (Japanese teacup saucers), shuki (sake cups), and many others. Making urushi lacquerware is a traditional Japanese craft and one of the symbols of Japan. People usually think that urushi lacquerware is mainly used for special occasions such as the New Year. But, in my parents' house, my mother loved urushi lacquerware and so we used it in our daily life, for example, bowls for miso soup and lunch boxes.

The lacquered soup bowl with my name on it that I have been using since childhood is my treasure. The more I realize the beauty of urushi lacquerware, the more I love it, and I visit urushi lacquerware craftsmen's workshops, or create urushi lacquerware which I design by myself. I now have quite a collection of lacquerware.

Urushi lacquerware is very delicate so it needs to be appropriately cared for, washed gently, and thoroughly wiped dry. But, if you use it carefully, it will last a lifetime. Besides being beautiful, it is functional in keeping warm food warm and cold food cold. These days, however, it is less used by the younger generation. I feel sad that the works of traditional Japanese craftsmanship, including the urushi lacquerware, are starting to disappear from our daily life.

Beautiful and functional tools can make our life happier and richer. I hope, even if only a little, people realize the greatness of urushi lacquerware and again use it in their daily life. We should never lose the skill required to make this distinguished Japanese handicraft and make sure it is handed down to the next generation.

だしみつ卵

Sweet dashi rolled omelet

見た目はシンプルですが、火加減にコツがあり、上手につくるのは意外とむずかしい料理です。四角いフライパンは卵焼き専用の道具ですが、丸いフライパンでも形を気にしなければつくれます。途中で多少くずれてもだんだん形が整ってくるので焦らなくて大丈夫。最後の一巻きが、きれいに焼ければ成功です。

This dish looks simple, but requires technique in adjusting the heat, and is in fact difficult to make. The square frying pan is exclusively for rolled omelets, but this dish can be made using round frying pans as well, if you don't mind the shape. Even if the layers don't line up during the process, there's no need to worry. If you can get the last layer rolled nicely, it will be a success.

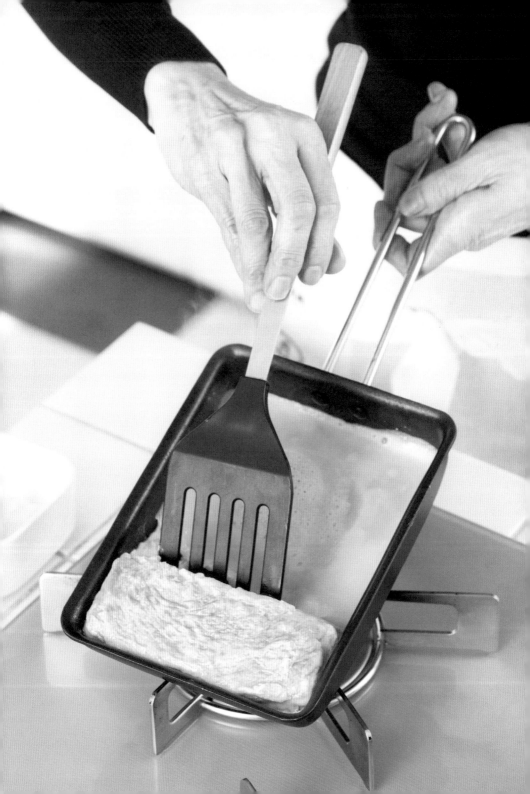

だしみつ卵

卵　6コ

［だしみつ］
砂糖　40g
だし　カップ1/2（100ml）
うす口しょうゆ　小さじ1
塩　少々

サラダ油　適宜

1. だしみつをつくる。温かいだしに砂糖を加えてよく溶かし、うす口しょうゆを加えて塩で味を調え、粗熱を取る。
2. ボウルに卵を溶きほぐし、だしみつを加えてよく混ぜ、一度こす。
3. 卵焼き用のフライパンにサラダ油を熱し、紙タオルなどでならして全体に油をなじませる。
4. 卵液を少量流し入れ、半熟のうちに手早く手前にまとめて芯にする。油が足りなければ3の要領でなじませ、再び卵液を流し入れ、芯の下にも行き渡るようにして巻き込む。これを数回繰り返す。
5. 焼き上がったら粗熱を取り、食べやすい大きさに切る。

Sweet dashi rolled omelet

[Makes 1 roll]

6 eggs

[sweet dashi sauce]
40g sugar
1/2 cup(100ml) dashi
1 tsp light soy sauce
salt

vegetable oil

1. Make the sweet dashi sauce: Add sugar in a warm dashi, and dissolve well. Add the light soy sauce, season with some salt, and let cool.

2. Beat the eggs in a bowl. Add the sweet dashi sauce, mix well, and strain.

3. Heat the omelet frying pan, and grease it with vegetable oil using a paper towel.

4. Pour a little egg mixture into the pan. Quickly pull it towards the edge of the pan while it is still half-cooked to create a center roll. If you need to add more oil to the pan, repeat the process in step 3. Add a little more egg mixture into the pan making sure that it flows under the center roll as well. Roll it towards the edge of the pan. Repeat this several times.

5. When it is done, let it cool, and cut it into bite-sized pieces.

もやしとねぎのあえそば

Noodles with shrimp and vegetables

わが家の簡単にできる人気おかずの一品。にんにくしょうがじょうゆはつくりおきしておくと、チャーハンなどいろんな料理に使えて便利です。香菜（シャンツァイ）と花椒（ホワジャオ）を加えるだけでぐっと本格的な味わいになって、驚くほどおいしい。

This is one of my family's favorite easy-to-make dishes. The garlic and ginger soy sauce would be nice to have on hand as it can be used for cooking a variety of dishes including fried rice. The added coriander leaves and Szechuan peppercorns give the dish an authentic Chinese taste, and make it surprisingly delicious.

もやしとねぎのあえそば

中国蒸し麺　2玉

むきえび　150g

もやし　1袋

長ねぎ　2本

にんにくしょうがじょうゆ
　　大さじ2

オイスターソース
　　大さじ1/2

サラダ油　適宜

紹興酒または酒　大さじ1/2

塩・こしょう　各適宜

ごま油　少々

香菜（シャンツァイ）　適宜

花椒(ホワジャオ)・
辛味酢（酢に赤とうがらしの
小口切りを加えたもの）　各適宜

[にんにくしょうがじょうゆ]

しょうゆ　カップ2（400ml）

にんにく　2～3かけ

しょうが　1かけ

にんにく、しょうがは薄切りに
する。広口瓶ににんにく、
しょうがを入れ、しょうゆを
加えて2～3時間以上おく。

1. えびは洗って背ワタがあれば取り除き、水けをふく。

2. もやしはひげ根を取り除く。

3. 長ねぎは5cm長さに切ってから縦に薄切りにする。

4. 麺は1本1本丁寧にほぐしておく。

5. にんにくしょうがじょうゆ、オイスターソースを混ぜ合わせておく。

6. フライパンにサラダ油大さじ1/2を熱し、えびを炒め、塩、こしょう、紹興酒をふり入れる。火が通ったらいったん取り出す。

7. 同じフライパンにサラダ油大さじ1を足し、麺を加えて炒め、取り出す。

8. 同じフライパンにサラダ油大さじ1～2を足し、もやしと長ねぎを強火で炒める。

9. えびと麺を戻し入れ、手早く混ぜる。火を止め、合わせた調味料を回しかけてあえ、塩、こしょう、ごま油で味を調える。

10. 器に盛り、すりつぶした花椒をふり、香菜、辛味酢を添える。

Noodles with shrimp and vegetables

[Serves 4]

---

2 portions steamed
  Chinese noodles

150g shelled shrimp

1 pack bean sprouts

2 Japanese leeks

2 tbsp garlic and
  ginger soy sauce

1/2 tbsp oyster sauce

vegetable oil

1/2 tbsp *shokoshu*
  (Chinese sake)
  or Japanese sake

salt and pepper

sesame oil

coriander leaves for garnish

Szechuan peppercorns,
  chopped red chili,
  vinegar --- to serve

[garlic and ginger soy sauce]

2 cups(400ml) soy sauce

2-3 cloves garlic

1 knob ginger

Slice the garlic and ginger
thinly. Put the garlic and
ginger in a jar and add the
soy sauce. Let it stand
for over 2 to 3 hours.

1. Rinse the shrimp and devein them if any. Pat them dry.

2. Remove the tails from the bean sprouts.

3. Cut the leeks into 5cm-long pieces and then slice thinly.

4. Gently pull the noodles apart one by one to loosen.

5. Combine the garlic and ginger soy sauce and oyster sauce in a bowl.

6. Heat 1/2 tbsp of oil in a frying pan and stir-fry the shrimp. Add the salt, pepper and *shokoshu*. Remove them from the pan once they are cooked.

7. Add 1 tbsp oil to the pan, add the noodles, and stir-fry. Remove them from the pan.

8. Add 1-2 tbsp oil to the pan and stir-fry the bean sprouts and leeks on high heat.

9. Put the shrimp and noodles back into the pan and stir. Turn off the heat and add the previously made sauce and toss them together. Add salt, pepper, and sesame oil to taste.

10. Pile onto a serving plate and sprinkle with ground Szechuan pepper and garnish with coriander leaves. Serve with vinegar mixed with chopped chili.

ざるそば

"Zaru soba"
(cold soba noodles)

めんつゆ

Mentsuyu (noodle broth)

ゆでて冷水できゅっとしめたそばとめんつゆ。薬味はねぎ、わさび、もみのりだけというシンプルな食べ方が好きです。このめんつゆは母から教えてもらった味。そばやうどんだけでなく、煮物に、丼にと便利に使い回しできるのでぜひ覚えておくといいです。

Soba, boiled and washed under cold running water, served with *mentsuyu*. The only garnishes are leek, wasabi and crumbled nori seaweed. I like the simple style of this dish. My mother taught me the recipe of this *mentsuyu*. It can be used not just for noodles, but also for many recipes such as simmered dishes or *donburi* (a bowl of rice topped with meat or vegetables and sauce). So this recipe will surely come in handy.

ざるそば

そば（乾）　200g

めんつゆ　適宜

もみのり　適宜

おろしわさび　適宜

長ねぎ　適宜
　（小口切りにして
　水にさらす）

1. 鍋にたっぷりの湯を沸かし、そばを
   ゆでる。くっつかないように、時々か
   き混ぜる。

2. 吹き上がってきたらカップ1程度の差
   し水をして沸騰をしずめ、ゆで上げる。

3. ざるにあけて流水でそばをよく洗い、
   水けをよくきる。

4. 器にそばを盛り、もみのりを散らす。
   めんつゆは別の碗に注ぐ。わさび、ね
   ぎを添える。

めんつゆ

水　カップ4（800ml）

しょうゆ
　カップ1+1/2（300ml）

みりん　カップ1（200ml）

砂糖　40g

削りがつお　50g

1. 鍋に分量の水、しょうゆ、みりんを合
   わせ、砂糖を加えて溶かす。

2. 火にかけ、沸騰する直前に削りがつ
   おを加え、弱めの中火で2〜3分煮
   立てたら火から下ろし、粗熱が取れ
   るまでそのままおく。

3. ざるでこし、冷蔵庫で冷やす。

　＊ 冷蔵庫で4〜5日保存できる。

"Zaru soba" (cold soba noodles)

[Serves 2]

200g dried
 soba noodles

mentsuyu

crumbled nori seaweed

grated wasabi

Japanese leek
 (chopped and soaked
 in water)
 --- for garnish

1. Bring plenty of water to a boil and add the soba. Stir the noodles occasionally to prevent them from sticking.

2. When the noodles are about to boil over, add 1 cup of water and continue boiling until the noodles are cooked through.

3. Drain and wash the noodles well under cold running water. Drain them well.

4. Put the noodles in serving plates and sprinkle crumbled nori seaweed on top. Pour the *mentsuyu* in separate serving bowls. Garnish with wasabi and Japanese leek.

Mentsuyu (noodle broth)

[Ingredients]

4 cups(800ml) water

1+1/2 cups(300ml)
 soy sauce

1 cup(200ml) mirin

40g sugar

50g bonito flakes

1. Combine the water, soy sauce, and mirin in a pan. Add the sugar and dissolve it.

2. Heat it until just before boiling. Add the bonito flakes and simmer over low heat for a few minutes. Remove from the heat and let it stand until it slightly cools.

3. Strain through a sieve and chill in the refrigerator.

  * *Mentsuyu* keeps in the refrigerator for 4-5 days.

ギョーザ

Gyoza
(Chinese dumplings)

ギョーザはわたしの大好きな料理のひとつ。中身はいろいろありますが、この具がいちばん好きです。水で溶いた小麦粉を入れ、底をパリッと焼いて、やけどしそうなほどアツアツなところを食べるのがおいしい。たっぷりのしょうがと酢じょうゆ、ラーユで食べて。

Gyoza is one of my favorite dishes. There are various fillings for *gyoza*, but this is my favorite recipe. By adding the water with a little flour when braising the *gyoza*, the bottoms get crispy. It's delicious to eat while they are still piping hot. Enjoy them with plenty of ginger, soy sauce with vinegar and chili oil.

ギョーザ

豚ひき肉　150g

白菜　150g

キャベツ　150g

にら（みじん切り）　50g

にんにく（みじん切り）
　大さじ1

紹興酒　大さじ1

スープ
　（中国風スープペースト
　小さじ1を湯大さじ1で溶き、
　冷ましたもの）

ごま油　適宜

サラダ油　少々

塩・こしょう　各適宜

ギョーザの皮　24枚

小麦粉　小さじ1

水　カップ1/2（100ml）

しょうゆ・酢・ラーユ　各適宜

しょうが（せん切り）　適宜

1. 白菜とキャベツはみじん切りにする。別々のボウルに入れ、それぞれ塩小さじ1ずつふってからめ、しばらくおく。しんなりとしたら水けをしっかり絞る。

2. フライパンにごま油大さじ1/2を熱し、にんにくのみじん切りを焦がさないように炒める。

3. ボウルに豚ひき肉を入れ、紹興酒、スープを加えて混ぜ合わせる。炒めたにんにくを油ごと加え、白菜、キャベツ、にらを入れて混ぜ、塩、こしょうで味を調え、ラップをして30分くらいねかせる。

4. ギョーザの皮にタネをスプーンなどですくってのせ、ふちに水をつけ、ひだを寄せながら閉じ合わせる。

5. 小麦粉は分量の水で溶いておく。

6. ギョーザを半量ずつ焼く。フライパンを熱してサラダ油少々を入れ、ギョーザを円く並べ入れ、少し焼く。小麦粉を溶いた水を半量注ぎ、ふたをして弱めの中火で蒸し焼きにする。水分がほとんどなくなったらごま油少々を回しかけ、ギョーザの底がカリッとするまで焼き、ひっくり返しながら皿に盛りつける。残りのギョーザも同様に焼く。ラーユ酢じょうゆ、しょうがのせん切りでいただく。

Gyoza (Chinese dumplings)

[Makes 24]

150g ground pork

150g *hakusai*
(Chinese cabbage)

150g cabbage

50g finely chopped *nira*
(Chinese chives)

1 tbsp chopped garlic

1 tbsp *shokoshu*
(Chinese sake)

soup (1 tsp Chinese soup
paste dissolved in 1 tbsp
hot water and cooled)

sesame oil

vegetable oil

salt and pepper

24 thin *gyoza* wrappers
(dumpling wrappers)

1 tsp flour

1/2 cup(100ml) water

soy sauce, vinegar,
chili oil ginger
(cut into fine trips)
--- to serve

1. Finely chop the *hakusai* and cabbage. Put them into separate bowls. Sprinkle 1tsp of salt into each bowl. Mix both of them lightly, and let stand for a while. Squeeze water out of the vegetables.

2. Put 1/2 tbsp sesame oil in a frying pan, and fry the chopped garlic.

3. Put the ground pork in a bowl. Add the *shokoshu* and soup, and mix together. Follow with the fried garlic, along with the oil, add the *hakusai*, cabbage, and *nira* and mix well. Season with some salt and pepper. Cover with plastic wrap and let it stand for 30 minutes.

4. Scoop the mixture onto a *gyoza* wrapper with a knife or spoon. Put the mixture on each *gyoza* wrapper. Wet the edges with a little water, fold it over, and pinch to seal.

5. Dissolve the flour with the water.

6. Pan-fry half of the dumplings at a time. Heat a frying pan and add some oil. Arrange the dumplings in a circle and cook for a short time. Pour half of the water with flour, cover with a lid, and cook over low-medium heat. When the water has almost evaporated, pour a little sesame oil around the dumplings, and cook until the bottoms of the dumplings get crisp. Turn over onto a plate and serve with soy sauce, vinegar, chili oil, and ginger.

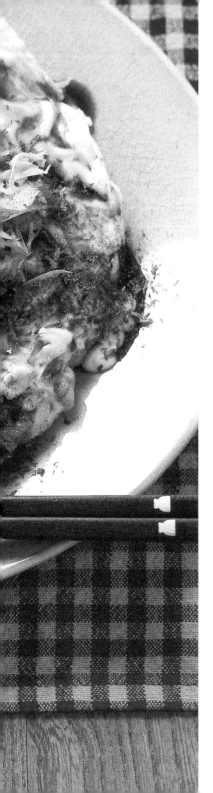

お好み焼き

Okonomiyaki
(savory Japanese pancakes)

お好み焼きは、外国の方につくるととても喜ばれる料理のひとつです。中の具は、ここで紹介するいか、えび、豚肉以外にも、好きなものを入れてつくってみてください。最後に散らすかつお節は、電子レンジ（200W）に5～6分かけてパリパリにしておくと、風味も出て一層おいしくなります。紅しょうがも欠かせません。

Okonomiyaki (literally 'your favorite things grilled') is one of the Japanese dishes that foreign people love. You can use any ingredients you like in place of the squid, shrimp, or pork that I introduce here. If you microwave (at 200W) the dried bonito flakes for about 5 to 6 minutes, it will become crispy and more flavorful. Sprinkle it over the *okonomiyaki* and add a little red pickled ginger for a delicious taste treat.

お好み焼き

いか（胴の部分）
　1ぱい分（120g）
えび　15匹（150g）
豚バラ肉（しゃぶしゃぶ用）
　200g
キャベツの葉　3枚（150g）
紅しょうが　大さじ2〜3
細ねぎ（小口切り）　カップ1/2
揚げ玉　大さじ2〜3
卵　4コ
サラダ油　適宜

[生地]
山芋　100g
卵　1コ
だし　カップ1（200ml）
小麦粉　カップ1（200ml）

[トッピング]
お好み焼きソース・マヨネーズ・
　青のり・かつお節　各適宜

1. いかは2cm角に切る。
2. えびは殻と尾を取り、横半分に切る。背ワタを取ってから、長さを2等分に切る。
3. 豚肉は4〜5cm長さに切る。
4. キャベツはせん切りにし、紅しょうがはみじん切りにする。
5. 山芋は皮をむいてすりおろす。
6. ボウルに卵1コ、だし、すりおろした山芋を入れて混ぜ合わせ、小麦粉を加えて軽く混ぜる。キャベツ、細ねぎ、揚げ玉、紅しょうがを加えて混ぜ、いかとえびを加える。
7. フライパンにサラダ油少々を熱し、お好み焼きの生地を1/4量（1人分）流し入れ、豚肉を広げてのせ、3〜4分焼く。裏返して火が通るまで焼く（3〜4分）。
8. 別のフライパンにサラダ油少々を熱し、卵1コを割り入れる。卵黄をつぶして軽くかき混ぜ、7を豚肉の面を下にしてのせて焼く。
9. 卵焼きの面を上にして皿にのせ、ソース、マヨネーズを順にぬり、青のり、かつお節をふる。残りの生地も同様に焼く。

Okonomiyaki (savory Japanese pancakes)

[Serves 4]

1 squid (body part, 120g)

15 shrimp (150g)

200g sliced pork belly
(for *shabushabu*)

3 cabbage leaves(150g)

2-3 tbsp red pickled ginger

1/2 cup chopped spring onion

2-3 tbsp *agedama*
(leftover fried tempura bits)

4 eggs

vegetable oil

[pancake batter]

100g *yamaimo* yam

1 egg

1 cup(200ml) dashi

1 cup(200ml) flour

[topping]

mayonnaise

okonomiyaki sauce
(a thick Worcester sauce)

aonori (green laver flakes)

dried bonito flakes

1. Cut the squid into 2cm-square pieces.
2. Remove the shells and tails from the shrimp. Slice them horizontally in half. Devein them, and cut in half lengthwise.
3. Cut the pork slices into 4-5cm strips.
4. Shred the cabbage. Chop the red ginger finely.
5. Peel and grate the *yamaimo*.
6. Mix 1 egg, dashi, and grated *yamaimo* in a bowl. Add the flour and stir lightly. Add the shredded cabbage, chopped spring onion, *agedama*, and red ginger, and combine. Add the squid and shrimp.
7. Heat a little oil in a frying pan. Pour in 1/4 of the batter (for 1 serving). Put the pork slices on top and cook for 3-4 minutes. Flip the pancake over and cook till ready (another 3-4 minutes).
8. Heat a little oil in another frying pan. Crack an egg into the pan. Stir the yolk lightly. Place the pancake from step 7 on top of the egg, pork side down, and continue cooking.
9. Turn it over onto a serving plate and spread *okonomiyaki* sauce and mayonnaise on top. Sprinkle with *aonori* and bonito flakes. Make 3 more *okonomiyaki* with the remaining batter in the same way.

まぐろのクロスティーニ

Tuna crostini

まぐろのヅケは昔からある日本の料理。その
まま食べてもおいしいのですが、パンにもよく
合うので、アボカドと合わせてイタリア料理の
前菜風に仕立ててみました。たれに加えたに
んにくの風味が味の決め手です。

Soy sauce-marinated tuna has been enjoyed in Japan since long ago. It's tasty as it
is, but it also goes well with bread, so I ar-
ranged it with avocado into a sort of an Ital-
ian appetizer. The garlic added in the sauce
makes it especially savory.

まぐろのクロスティーニ

まぐろ（刺身用・赤身または中トロ）
　1サク（150g）
にんにく　小1かけ
しょうゆ　大さじ2
酒　大さじ2

［アボカドクリーム］
アボカド　1コ
レモン汁　少々
オリーブ油　大さじ1
塩・こしょう　各少々

きゅうり　1/2本
バゲット（2cm厚さのスライス）
　8〜10切れ

1. にんにくは薄くスライスする。
2. 鍋に湯を沸かし、沸騰したところにまぐろを入れて15秒ゆで、すぐに氷水に浸して冷ます。熱が取れたら紙タオルで水分を丁寧にふく。
3. 保存容器にしょうゆと酒を合わせ、まぐろをつけ、にんにくを入れて冷蔵庫に2〜3時間おく。食べる直前に汁けをきって5〜8mm厚さに切る。
4. アボカドは半分に切って種を除き、スプーンでくりぬいてボウルに入れ、つぶす。レモン汁、オリーブ油を加え混ぜ、塩、こしょうで味を調える。
5. きゅうりは縦に薄くスライスする。
6. 焼き網を熱し、バゲットをこんがりと焼き色がつくまで焼く。アボカドクリームを全体にぬり、きゅうりをのせ、汁けをきったまぐろとにんにくをのせる。好みで上からオリーブ油をかける。

Tuna crostini

---

1 block (150g) tuna
(for sashimi / lean meat
or medium fatty flesh)

1 small clove garlic

2 tbsp soy sauce

2 tbsp sake

[avocado cream]

1 avocado

squeezed lemon juice

1 tbsp olive oil

salt, pepper

1/2 cucumber

8-10 slices baguette
(each 2cm-thick)

1. Cut the garlic into thin slices.
2. Bring a pot of water to a boil, put the tuna in and boil for 15 seconds. Take out the tuna and immediately soak in ice water to cool. When cooled, drain, and wipe thoroughly with a paper towel.
3. Combine the soy sauce with sake in a food storage container, marinate the tuna in it, top it with garlic slices and chill in the refrigerator for 2-3 hours. Drain the tuna and cut into 5-8mm-thick slices just before eating.
4. Halve and stone the avocado. Using a spoon, scoop out the flesh into a bowl and mash. Add lemon juice and olive oil and mix. Season with salt and pepper.
5. Thinly slice the cucumber lengthwise.
6. Heat the grill and toast the baguette until crispy brown. Apply avocado cream evenly to the surface, and lay the cucumber slices. Top it with drained tuna and garlic slices. Sprinkle olive oil if preferred.

こねないパン

No-knead bread

わたしはオーブンから出てきた焼きたての
アツアツのパンが大好きです。自分で焼く
と多少うまくいかなくてもアツアツが食べ
られるので幸せな気分になります。このパ
ンは時間はかかりますが、こねないので気
楽につくることができます。生地にチーズや
レーズン、木の実などを入れていろいろな
味を楽しんでください。

I love piping hot bread, fresh out of the
oven. This is the advantage of baking
your own bread. Even if it's not done per-
fectly, you can still enjoy the bliss of eating a freshly baked one. This recipe is a
bit time-consuming, but there's no need to
knead, so it doesn't require special skills.
Feel free to experiment with the recipe by
adding different ingredients to the dough,
such as cheese, raisins, and nuts.

こ ね な い パ ン

強力粉　300g

砂糖　小さじ2

塩　小さじ1/2

インスタントドライイースト
　小さじ1

水　200ml
　（水温は25℃前後
　のものを使用）

打ち粉（強力粉）　適宜

1. ボウルに強力粉を入れ、砂糖、塩、ドライイーストを別々にのせてからよく混ぜる。水を入れ、木べらで粉けがなくなるまでよく混ぜ、ひとつにまとめてラップをし、約2時間おいて発酵させる（一次発酵）。もとの大きさのおよそ2倍に膨らむまでが目安。

   * 冬場など、気温の低い時期は発酵に時間がかかるのでオーブンの発酵機能で30〜35℃で発酵させてもよい。

2. 生地が膨らんだら生地とボウルの間に打ち粉をして、カードで縁から生地を取り出して両手で持つ。台には置かずに手のひらでひとつにまとめ、打ち粉を足しながら両手で生地を引っ張るように丸め、何度か繰り返してガス抜きする。なめらかにしながら丸く形を整え、下の部分をしっかり閉じてボウルに戻してラップをし、さらに約1時間おいて発酵させる（二次発酵）。

3. 鍋にオーブン用の紙を敷き、もう一度、2と同様に生地を丸く整えて置き、表面に軽く打ち粉をしてふたをし、さらに約1時間おいて鍋の中で生地が1.5倍くらいになるまでおいて発酵させる（三次発酵）。

4. オーブンを200℃に予熱する。

5. 天板に鍋をのせ、ふたをしたまま約30分焼く。生地が十分に膨らんだらふたを外し、さらに200℃で約30分焼き、こんがりと焼き色がついたら取り出して網の上で粗熱を取る。または焼きたてにバターなどをつけていただく。

No-knead bread

300g bread flour

2 tsp sugar

1/2 tsp salt

1 tsp instant
dry yeast

200ml water
(around 25°C)

bread flour
for dusting

1. Put the bread flour into a bowl, add sugar, salt, dry yeast separately in that order, and mix well. Pour in the room-temperature water, and stir well with a wooden spoon until all the flour mixture is incorporated. Form into a ball in the bowl, cover with plastic wrap and let rise for about 2 hours. (primary fermentation) The dough should rise to about double the original size.

   * When the room temperature is low, such as during the winter season, fermentation takes longer. You can use the fermentation function of the oven at around 30-35°C

2. When the dough has risen, dust some flour between the dough and the bowl, scrape out the dough with dough scraper from the edges of the bowl, hold the dough in both hands. Shape the dough into a ball in your palms, stretch it out, and shape it into a ball again, while dusting more flour. Repeat this process several times to let the gas out. Smooth out the surface and shape into a ball. Return the dough to the bowl seam-side down, cover with plastic wrap and let stand for about an hour. (secondary fermentation)

3. Line the pot with parchment paper. Repeat the process in step 2 and shape the dough into a ball. Dust the surface with flour and place it into the pot and put on the lid. Let it rest in the pot for about another hour until the dough rises to one and a half times the original size. (third fermentation)

4. Preheat the oven to 200°C.

5. Place the pot in the oven and bake for 30 minutes with the lid on. When the dough has risen sufficiently, remove the lid and bake for another 30 minutes at 200°C. When the surface turns golden brown, take it out of the oven onto a rack and let it cool down. Serve with butter etc. fresh out of the oven.

豚汁

Pork and vegetable miso soup

豚汁は日本のだれもが好き
な料理。野菜のいろんな切
り方が学べるので、子ども
たちに料理を教えるとき、よ
く豚汁をつくります。

This is a favorite dish of
the Japanese. You can learn
various ways to cut vegetables, so I often choose this
dish when teaching cook-
ing to children.

豚 汁

大根　5cm（200g）

にんじん　5cm（100g）

ごぼう　1/2本（100g）

こんにゃく　1枚（200g）

里芋　2〜3コ（180g）

豚バラ薄切り肉　200g

だし　カップ6（1200ml）

みそ　大さじ5〜6

長ねぎ　少々
　（小口切りにして
　水にさらす）

七味とうがらし　適宜

1. 大根とにんじんは皮をむいて5mm厚さのいちょう切りにする。

2. ごぼうは皮をむいてささがきにし、水にさらしてアクを抜き、水けをきる。

3. こんにゃくは一口大にちぎり、下ゆでしてざるに上げる。

4. 里芋は皮をむいて輪切り、または半月切りにし、水にさらして水けをよくきる。

5. 豚肉は一口大に切る。

6. 鍋にだしを熱し、大根、にんじん、ごぼう、こんにゃく、里芋を加える。煮立ったらアクを取って弱火にする。

7. 野菜が柔らかくなったら豚肉を加える。肉に火が通ったらみそを溶き入れる。

8. 器に盛り、長ねぎの小口切りをのせる。好みで七味とうがらしを添える。

Pork and vegetable miso soup

[Serves 4]

5cm daikon(200g)

5cm carrot(100g)

1/2 burdock(100g)

1 piece konnyaku(200g)

2-3 taroes(180g)

200g thinly sliced pork ribs

6 cups(1200ml) dashi

5-6 tbsp miso

Japanese leek, chopped and soaked in water, *shichimi* pepper --- for garnish

1. Peel the daikon and carrot, cut them in quarters lengthwise, and slice them into 5mm-thick quarter-rounds(*icho-giri*). (see page 280)

2. Peel the burdock and shave it into *sasagaki* slices. (see page 284) Soak the burdock in cold water to remove the bitterness, then drain.

3. Tear the konnyaku into bite-sized pieces. Boil it in water to remove the bitterness, then drain.

4. Peel the taro and cut horizontally into *wagiri* or *hangetsu-giri* pieces (rounds or half-moons). Soak in water, then drain.

5. Cut the pork into bite-sized pieces.

6. Heat the dashi in a pot, and add the daikon, carrot, burdock, konnyaku and taro. Skim the surface when the broth comes to a boil. Lower the heat.

7. When the vegetables become soft, add the pork. When the pork is cooked through, dissolve the miso into the broth.

8. Pour in a serving bowl and garnish with chopped leek. Serve with *shichimi* pepper to taste.

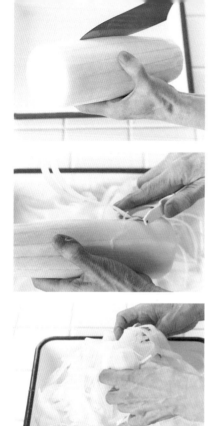

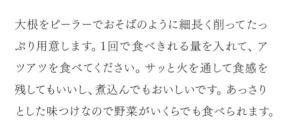

大根をピーラーでおそばのように細長く削ってたっぷり用意します。1回で食べきれる量を入れて、アツアツを食べてください。サッと火を通して食感を残してもいいし、煮込んでもおいしいです。あっさりとした味つけなので野菜がいくらでも食べられます。

Shave the daikon with a peeler into plenty of noodle-like strips. Put only the amount you can eat at one time into the pot, and enjoy it while it's still piping hot. You can enjoy the texture of the daikon if you take it out of the soup quickly. It also tastes good when it has been simmered well. It is lightly flavored, so you can eat plenty of vegetables without feeling heavy in the stomach.

大根そば鍋

Daikon noodle pot

大 根 そ ば 鍋

豚肉（しゃぶしゃぶ用）
（肩ロース / バラなど）
300〜400g

大根　20cm長さ
（正味約500g）

クレソン　3ワ

［煮汁］
だし　カップ8（1600ml）
うす口しょうゆ　大さじ2
しょうゆ　大さじ2
酒　大さじ2
塩　小さじ1

ゆず　適宜
七味とうがらし　適宜
粉ざんしょう　適宜

1. 大根は皮をむき、縦に1.5cm間隔で切り目を入れ、ピーラーで麺のように長く削る。
2. クレソンは洗って水けをよくきり、下の堅い部分を少し落として半分の長さに切る。
3. 鍋に煮汁のだしと調味料を入れて煮立て、大根を入れて火を通し、豚肉を広げながら加える。最後にクレソンを加えてサッと火を通し、器に取り分ける。ゆずを絞り、好みで七味とうがらし、粉ざんしょうなどをかけていただく。

Daikon noodle pot

[Serves 4]

300-400g pork
  for *shabushabu*
  (shoulder loin/rib etc.)
20cm piece daikon
  (about 500g)
3 bundles watercress

[broth]
8 cups (1600ml) dashi
2 tbsp light soy sauce
2 tbsp soy sauce
2 tbsp sake
1 tsp salt

yuzu
shichimi pepper
sansho powder --- to taste

1. Peel the daikon, make incisions along the length of the daikon at 1.5cm intervals, then shave the daikon using a peeler to make noodle-like strips.

2. Wash the watercress and drain well. Trim the woody stem ends, and cut in half.

3. Combine the ingredients for the broth in a pan and heat it. When it comes to a boil, add the daikon and let it cook, and then add the pork while spreading out each piece. Finally, add the watercress just before turning off the heat. Put it in a serving bowl, squeeze some yuzu over it, and garnish with *shichimi* or *sansho* powder if preferred.

ゆず ｜ Yuzu

れんこんやごぼうなどの根菜、小松菜や水菜などの青菜、せり、みょうがなどの香り野菜、ゆずやすだちなどのかんきつ類…。好きなものを挙げたらきりがありませんが、どれも大好きな日本の味で、わたしの料理には欠かせないものばかりです。中でも、ゆずは1年でもっとも待ちわびる季節の香り。手に入る時期には、レモンと同じように、肉や魚、野菜などに直接搾って使っています。皮は、ほんの少し添えるだけでもぐっと料理を引き立ててくれますが、たっぷり刻んで入れられるのも、その時期ならではのぜいたく。また、果汁をしょうゆと合わせたゆずしょうゆは、鍋のたれに、あえ物に、炒め物にと、何にでも使えるわが家の大切な調味料なので、季節になると一年分をつくり、冷蔵庫と冷凍庫で保存します。

日本料理がポピュラーになるにつれて、海外でも日本の食材が手に入りやすくなってきましたが、それでもこうした四季折々の食材は、なかなか入手しづらいもの。海外に向けてレシピを紹介するときは、なるべくたくさんの人に気軽につくってほしいと思うので、手に入りやすい食材でつくれるようにアレンジしていますが、その一方で、こうした日本の食材のすばらしさを、もっともっと知ってもらいたいとも思います。もし手に入る機会があったらぜひ試して、その魅力に触れていただけたらうれしいです。

【ゆず】

かんきつ類の一種で、熟してから収穫する黄ゆず(秋から冬に出回る)と、未熟果を収穫する青ゆず(初夏から初秋に出回る)がある。独特のさわやかな香りが特徴。果肉は酸味が非常に強いため、直接食用とすることはないが、果汁は料理に香りや酸味を加えるために調味料として使われる。果皮は薄く切って、料理の香りづけによく用いられる。皮の内側の白い部分は苦みがあるので、皮を使うときは表面だけ薄く包丁でそぎ取って使う。料理のほか、冬には風呂に入れて香りを楽しんだりもする。

Root vegetables including lotus root and burdock, green vegetables including *komatsuna* and *mizuna*, flavorful vegetables including *seri* and *myoga*, and citrus fruits including yuzu and sudachi – I have so many favorite Japanese ingredients. They are all essential to my recipes.

Among them, yuzu is the flavor whose season I look forward to the most. During its season, I directly squeeze yuzu on meat, fish, and vegetables as you would a lemon. Even a tiny zest of yuzu can enhance the original taste of the dish, but I enjoy the luxury of using plenty of shredded yuzu zest when it's in season. Yuzu soy sauce, a mixture of yuzu juice and soy sauce, is an important seasoning in my family – we use it for all sorts of dishes, from dipping sauce for hot-pots to vegetable dressing and stir-fried food. During its season, I make enough yuzu soy sauce for one year and preserve it in the refrigerator and freezer.

The more Japanese food has become popular internationally, the easier it has become to find Japanese ingredients overseas. However, such seasonal ingredients as yuzu remain difficult to obtain. When I introduce recipes to people living outside Japan, I usually arrange the recipes with ingredients they can easily obtain, because I hope as many people as possible will try and enjoy this style of cooking without any difficulty. But on the other hand, I hope more and more people realize how delicious these Japanese seasonal ingredients are. I would be happy if you should find an opportunity to taste them and experience the pleasure of these seasonal foods.

....

【Yuzu】

Yuzu is a kind of citrus fruit. There are two types of yuzu: yellow yuzu, from autumn to winter, is harvested when the fruit is ripe; and green yuzu, from early summer to early autumn, is harvested before the fruit is ripe. Yuzu has a unique fresh aroma. The flesh is so sour that it is not eaten, but the juice is used as a seasoning to add aroma and tartness to dishes. Thinly shaved slices of the zest are also used for flavor. As the white part beneath the zest is very bitter, only the surface of the zest is shaved and used. This fruit is not only for cooking – people also put yuzu in their bathtub and enjoy its aroma in wintertime.

4

DESERTS

甘味

わたしの仕事はみんなでお茶とお菓子を楽
しむところから始まります。まだテレビの裏
方の仕事をしていたときから、いつか料理家
になったら朝のお茶の時間を大事にしようと
思っていました。いつか来るその日のために
と、たくさん練習したのがこのシフォンケーキ。
今でもこれをつくると当時を思い出し、これ
までがんばってきてよかったと思うと同時に、
もっとおいしくつくらなければと思います。

My work day begins by enjoying a cup of
tea and some sweets with my coworkers. I
started out as a staff member working be-
hind the scenes for a TV cooking show. But
even back then, I had been telling myself
that I would cherish morning teatime if I
ever became a cooking writer. It was this
chiffon cake that I had been practicing
many times in anticipation of that day. Even
now, when I make this cake, it reminds me
of those days, and I feel glad that I have
come this far. At the same time, it makes me
more determined to make it even better.

スパイスシフォンケーキ

Chiffon cake

スパイスシフォンケーキ

【 材料 直径24cmの大型 1台分 】

薄力粉　カップ2（約220g）
ベーキングパウダー　大さじ1
卵　大10コ
グラニュー糖　カップ1（約180g）
サラダ油　カップ1/2（100ml）
水　カップ1/2（100ml）

[スパイス]
シナモンパウダー　大さじ1/2〜1
オールスパイス　小さじ1
クローブ　小さじ1
キャラウェイシード　大さじ2

粉砂糖　適宜

[下準備] オーブンは170℃に温めておく。

1. 卵は卵黄と卵白に分ける。

2. 卵黄にグラニュー糖の半量を入れて混ぜ、泡立て器でもったりするまでよく混ぜる。

3. サラダ油と水を順に加えてよく混ぜる。

4. 薄力粉、ベーキングパウダーを合わせたものをふるい入れ、泡立て器でサックリと混ぜ、スパイスを入れて生地に粉っぽさがなくなり、なめらかになるまで混ぜ合わせる。

5. メレンゲをつくる。別のボウルに卵白をハンドミキサーで六分立てに泡立て、残りのグラニュー糖を加えてツノがしっかりと立つまで堅く泡立てる。

6. 4に5の1/3量を入れてゴムべらでよく混ぜ合わせ、残りのメレンゲを2回くらいに分けて加え、白いところがなくなるまで手早く混ぜる。

7. 生地を少し高い位置から型に流し入れる。

8. 型ごとトントンと2〜3回、台に打ちつけて余分な空気を抜く。

9. 170℃のオーブンで45〜55分焼いて取り出し、逆さにして蒸れないように型の中央を容器で支え、よく冷ます。

10. ナイフを差し込んで、型を傷つけないように丁寧に型から外し、底の部分も外す。

11. 食べやすく切って器に盛り、好みで粉砂糖をふる。

Chiffon cake

2 cups (220g) flour

1 tbsp baking powder

10 eggs (large)

1 cup (180g) granulated sugar

1/2 cup (100ml) vegetable oil

1/2 cup (100ml) water

[spices]

1/2-1 tbsp cinnamon powder

1 tsp allspice

1 tsp clove

2 tbsp caraway seed

powdered sugar

[preparation] Preheat the oven to 170°C.

1. Separate the eggs into yolks and whites.

2. Add half of the granulated sugar into egg yolks and beat well with a whisk until it thickens.

3. Add first the vegetable oil and then the water and mix well.

4. Sift together the flour and baking powder, mix lightly with a whisk. Add the spices and mix well until all the flour mixture is incorporated and the batter is smooth.

5. Make the meringue: In a separate bowl, beat the egg whites with a hand mixer until soft peaks form. Add the rest of the granulated sugar and beat until it forms hard peaks.

6. Add a third of the meringue in step 5 into the egg yolk mixture in step 4. Fold with a rubber spatula. Repeat the same process with the rest of the meringue, and fold quickly until the color of the mixture is uniform.

7. Pour the batter into the tube pan from a slightly higher place.

8. Lift the pan and drop onto the counter several times to help release air bubbles from the batter.

9. Bake for 45-55 minutes in a preheated 170°C oven. Take it out of the oven and flip the pan over to let the cake cool completely upside down. Support the center hole of the pan with a container so as not to let the cake sweat.

10. Carefully run a knife around the edges making sure not to scratch the pan, and take the cake out of the pan gently.

11. Cut the cake into serving-size pieces, and serve on a plate. Sprinkle with powdered sugar to taste.

パンナコッタ

Panna cotta

昔からつくっているうちの定番のデザートです。ほんのりとラム酒の風味がきいた大人の味。ゼラチンの量は固まるぎりぎりにして、とろけるような柔らかな食感にこだわりました。どんな人にも喜んでもらえる味です。

I have been making this dessert for a long time, and it is one of my family's favorites. The rum gives it a more adult flavor. I use minimum amount of gelatin to give it a creamy texture that melts in your mouth. This is a dessert everyone loves.

パンナコッタ

【 材料 小8〜10コ分 】

牛乳　カップ1+1/2（300ml）
バニラビーンズ　1/2本
グラニュー糖　60g
粉ゼラチン　1袋（5g）
水　大さじ2
生クリーム　カップ1（200ml）
ラム酒　大さじ2

［カラメルソース］
グラニュー糖　50g
水　小さじ1
湯　カップ1/4（50ml）

1. 小さいボウルに分量の水を入れ、ゼラチンをふり入れてふやかす。

2. 鍋に牛乳を入れる。バニラビーンズはさやを縦半分に切って種を取り出し、さやと種を鍋に加えて弱火にかける。グラニュー糖を加えて溶かす。

3. 沸騰直前に火を止める。バニラのさやを取り出し、ふやかしたゼラチンを残さず加え、混ぜながら溶かす。

4. 生クリームを少しずつ加えて混ぜ、ラム酒を加えて風味をつける。

5. 鍋底を氷水に当て、軽くとろみがつくまでしばらく混ぜながら冷やす。

6. 器に流し入れ、冷蔵庫で冷やし固める。

7. カラメルソースをつくる。小鍋にグラニュー糖と水を入れて火にかける。少し色づいたら鍋ごと揺り動かし、薄いカラメル色になるまで弱火で加熱する。火を止めて湯を加え、十分に冷めたら、パンナコッタに添える。

Panna cotta

1+1/2 cups (300ml) milk

1/2 vanilla bean

60g granulated sugar

1 pack (5g) gelatin powder

2 tbsp water

1 cup (200ml) heavy cream

2 tbsp rum

[caramel sauce]

50g granulated sugar

1 tsp water

1/4 cup (50ml) hot water

1. Sprinkle gelatin powder evenly over 2 tbsp water in a small bowl, and let it soften.

2. Put the milk in a pan. Split the vanilla bean pod lengthways and scrape out the seeds. Put the pod and the seeds into the pan and cook over low heat. Add granulated sugar and let it dissolve.

3. Turn the heat off just before it comes to a boil. Take out the vanilla pod, and add all of the softened gelatin. Mix and let it dissolve.

4. Add the heavy cream little by little while mixing. Add flavor with a spritz of rum.

5. Prepare a bowl full of ice water, cool the pan on top of it, mix and cool until it slightly thickens.

6. Pour the mixture into each container and chill in the refrigerator until it sets.

7. Make the caramel sauce: Put the granulated sugar and water in a small pan and heat. When the color starts to change, shake the pan and cook over low heat until it turns light amber. Turn off the heat, and add the hot water. When it cools, pour the sauce over the panna cotta.

小倉アイスクリーム

Ogura ice cream

卵がたっぷり入ったバニラアイスクリームに市販のゆで小豆を加えた和風のデザート。ベースのバニラアイスのつくり方だけ覚えたら、小豆のほかにいちごやブルーベリー、ラズベリーなどのフルーツを混ぜて、いろんなバリエーションのアイスクリームが楽しめます。

This is a Japanese-style dessert, made by adding store-bought boiled azuki beans to vanilla ice cream that contains lots of egg. All you have to do is to learn how to make the basic vanilla ice cream. Then, you will be able to enjoy various flavors by adding fruit, such as strawberries, blueberries, and raspberries instead of azuki beans.

小倉アイスクリーム

卵　2コ
グラニュー糖　50g
生クリーム　カップ1（200ml）
粒あん（市販）　100g
ゆで小豆（市販）　200g

1. ボウルに卵を入れて溶きほぐし、グ
   ラニュー糖の半量を加えて泡立て器
   でよくすり混ぜる。
2. 別のボウルに生クリームと残りのグ
   ラニュー糖を加えて堅く泡立てる。
3. 2に1を加えて混ぜる。バットなどに
   流し入れ、ラップをして冷凍庫に入
   れ、途中で固まりかけたら粒あんと
   ゆで小豆を加える。再び冷凍庫に戻
   し、さらに2〜3度混ぜながら冷や
   し固める。

Ogura ice cream

2 eggs

50g granulated sugar

1 cup (200ml) heavy cream

100g sweet azuki bean paste with skin (store-bought)

200g boiled azuki beans (store-bought)

1. Beat the eggs in a bowl, add half of the granulated sugar and mix well using a whisk.

2. Pour the heavy cream into a separate bowl, add the rest of the granulated sugar and whisk until you reach stiff peaks.

3. Add the mixture in step 1 into step 2. Pour the mixture into a shallow container, cover with plastic wrap and put in the freezer. As it starts to freeze, take it out of the freezer and mix in the azuki bean paste and the beans, put it back in the freezer. Stir the mixture several times while it freezes.

母ドーナツ

Mom's doughnuts

昔、母から教わった思い出のドー
ナツです。お菓子はあまりつくら
ない母でしたが、このドーナツは
父が好きだったこともあってよく
くってくれました。生地がとても柔
らかいですが、これがびっくりする
ほどおいしくできるのです。

My mother taught me how to
make these doughnuts a long time
ago. And it brings back memories.
My mother didn't make many
sweets, but she often made these
doughnuts because they were my
father's favorite. The very loose
dough is the secret to making
surprisingly delicious doughnuts.

母ドーナツ

【 材料（リング型・ボール型 各10コ分）】

卵　2コ

砂糖（上白糖）　80g

牛乳　カップ1/4（50ml）

バター　40g

薄力粉　250g

ベーキングパウダー
　小さじ2

打ち粉（強力粉）　適宜

揚げ油　適宜

砂糖（上白糖。
　仕上げ用）　適宜

シナモンパウダー　適宜

1. バターは溶かしバターにする。小さい耐熱容器に入れてふわっとラップをし、電子レンジ（600W）に約30秒かける。

2. ボウルに卵を割り入れ、泡立て器で溶きほぐし、砂糖を加えて混ぜる。

3. 牛乳と溶かしバターを加え、さらによく混ぜる。

4. 薄力粉、ベーキングパウダーを合わせてふるい入れ、ゴムべらで全体がなめらかになるまで混ぜる。

5. 打ち粉をふったオーブン用の紙の上に4の生地をのせ、1.5cm厚さにのばし、上からも打ち粉をふって、ふわっとラップをかけて冷蔵庫で生地が堅くなるまで3時間以上休ませる。

6. 生地を取り出し、抜き型に1回ごとに粉をつけながら抜く。生地が柔らかいので、丁寧に扱う。

7. 約180℃に熱した揚げ油に入れ、焦げないように返しながらこんがりと全体で2分〜2分30秒揚げ、中まで火を通す。火の通りの早い小さいボールから先に取り出す。

8. 仕上げ。プレーンタイプは、揚げたてに砂糖をたっぷりまぶす。シナモンタイプは、砂糖をまぶしてからシナモンパウダーをふる。

Mom's doughnuts

[Makes 10 ring doughnuts and 10 doughnut holes]

2 eggs

80g sugar
  (refined white sugar)

1/4 cup (50ml) milk

40g butter

250g flour

2 tsp baking powder

bread flour for dusting

oil for deep-frying

sugar (refined white sugar),
  cinnamon powder
  --- for sprinkling on top

1. Melt the butter by placing in a small heat-resistant container, cover loosely with a plastic wrap, and microwave (600W) for about 30seconds.

2. Crack the eggs in a bowl. Whisk them, add the sugar and mix well.

3. Add the milk and melted butter and continue to mix well.

4. Sift flour and baking powder into the mixture, and mix well with a rubber spatula until smooth.

5. Place the dough on step 4 on floured parchment paper. Roll it out to a thickness of 1.5cm. Dust some more flour from the top, and loosely cover it with a plastic wrap. Let it rest in the refrigerator for more than 3 hours until the dough hardens.

6. Take out the dough from the fridge, cut with a floured doughnut cutter. Flour the cutter each time. The dough is very soft, so treat with care.

7. Heat oil to around 180°C, and deep-fry the doughnuts. Turn them over so as not to overcook them, and deep-fry for 2 to 2-and-a half minutes until they are golden brown and cooked through. Take out the smaller doughnut holes that are done first.

8. Topping: For the plain doughnuts, sprinkle plenty of sugar while still hot. For the cinnamon ones, sprinkle cinnamon powder after they have been sprinkled with sugar.

ふわふわパンケーキ

Fluffy pancakes

メレンゲを加えてふわふわに焼き上げたパンケーキ。卵白を泡立てるというひと手間がありますが、それだけの価値があります。ハワイの大学でこのパンケーキを教えたとき、皆さんに「こんなにおいしいのを食べたのは初めて」と言われ、うれしかったのを覚えています。

These pancakes are especially fluffy because of the added meringue. Whipping up the egg whites is a bit of work, but it's definitely worth it. When I taught this recipe at the college in Hawaii, everybody told me they had never tasted pancakes this good. I remember how happy I was to hear that.

ふわふわパンケーキ

プレーンヨーグルト（無糖）
　　カップ1/2（100ml）

卵　2コ

グラニュー糖　30g

牛乳　カップ1/4（50ml）

薄力粉　100g

ベーキングパウダー　小さじ1

サラダ油またはバター　少々

バター　適宜

好みのジャム　適宜

メープルシロップ　適宜

1. ボウルにざるを重ねて紙タオルを敷き、ヨーグルトを入れる。ラップをし、冷蔵庫に1時間以上おいて水けをきる。

2. 卵は卵黄と卵白に分ける。

3. 卵黄にグラニュー糖の1/3量を加え、泡立て器でよくすり混ぜる。水けをきったヨーグルト、牛乳を加えてさらによく混ぜる。

4. 卵白に残りのグラニュー糖を加え、ハンドミキサーでツノが立つまでよく泡立てる。

5. 3に薄力粉とベーキングパウダーを合わせてふるい入れ、ゴムべらで混ぜる。

6. 5に4の1/3量を加えて混ぜる。さらに残りの4を加え、泡を消さないようにサックリと混ぜる。

7. フライパンを火にかけてサラダ油またはバターを熱し、生地の1/4量を流し入れる。火を弱めてふたをし、端が焼けてきたら裏返し、中まで火を通す。残り3枚も同様に焼く。

8. 焼きたてを器に盛り、バター、好みのジャム、メープルシロップを添える。

Fluffy pancakes

1/2 cup (100ml)
   plain yogurt
   (unsweetened)

2 eggs

30g granulated sugar

1/4 cup(50ml) milk

100g flour

1 tsp baking powder

vegetable oil or butter

butter, jam, maple syrup
   --- for toppings

1. Place a colander in a bowl and line them with a paper towel. Put the yogurt in it and cover with plastic wrap. Let it stand for at least an hour in the refrigerator to drain the yogurt.

2. Separate the eggs into yolks and whites.

3. Add a third of the sugar to the yolks and mix well with a whisk. Add the drained yogurt and milk and mix well.

4. Add the remaining sugar to the egg whites and whisk with a hand mixer until it makes stiff peaks.

5. Mix the flour and baking powder and sift it into the mixture in step 3. Fold with a rubber spatula.

6. Add a third of the mixture in step 4 into step 5, and mix. Add the remaining mixture and fold gently so as not to deflate the egg whip.

7. Heat some vegetable oil or butter in a frying pan, pour in a quarter of the batter. Lower the heat and put on a lid. When the edges are cooked, flip it over and cook through. Repeat this process with the remaining batter.

8. Serve fresh out of the pan with toppings of your choice, such as butter, jam or maple syrup.

失敗しないチーズケーキ

Fail-proof cheese cake

お菓子づくりはむずかしいというイメージがありますが、このチーズケーキは1つのボウルに材料を混ぜて焼くだけ。初めての人でも必ず上手につくれます。プレゼントにすることも多く、庭のハーブを小さなブーケにして添えています。

People tend to think that baking sweets is difficult. But with this cheese cake, all you have to do is to mix the ingredients into one bowl and bake. It will come out delicious, even if you are baking it for the first time. I often give it out as a present, decorating it with a tiny bouquet of herbs from my garden.

失敗しないチーズケーキ

【 材料 直径18cmの底が抜けるタイプの丸型 1台分 】

クリームチーズ　1箱（200g）

バター　30g
　（食塩不使用でも有塩でもよい）

ビスケット
　（全粒粉タイプのもの）　100g

グラニュー糖　カップ1/2（90g）

卵　2コ

生クリーム　カップ1（200ml）

薄力粉　大さじ3

レモン汁　大さじ1

粉砂糖　適宜

［下準備］

クリームチーズはボウルに入れて室温に戻しておく。

バターも室温に戻しておく。

型に合わせて底と側面にオーブン用の紙を敷く。

オーブンは160〜170℃に温めておく。

1. ビスケットをポリ袋に入れ、すりこ木など
   で粗くつぶし、バターと混ぜ合わせる。型
   の底に入れ、ポリ袋を裏返して手を入れ、
   押さえて敷き詰める。

2. ボウルにクリームチーズを入れ、ハンドミキ
   サーで混ぜてなめらかにする。

3. グラニュー糖、卵を順に加えてよく混ぜる。

4. 生クリームを加え、もったりするまでさらに
   よく混ぜ合わせる。

5. 薄力粉をふるい入れ、ゴムべらで軽く混ぜ、
   レモン汁を加えてさらに混ぜる。

6. 型に流し入れ、型の周囲を持って持ち上げ、
   台に2〜3度軽く落として空気を抜き、温
   めておいたオーブンで40〜45分焼く。

7. 取り出して粗熱を取り、型から外し、冷蔵
   庫で冷やす。

   ＊ 焼いたチーズケーキは冷凍保存できる。

8. 食べやすく切り分け、好みで粉砂糖をふる。

Fail-proof cheese cake

[18cm round cake pan with removable bottom / makes 1]

1 box (200g)
  cream cheese

30g butter
  (salted or unsalted)

100g biscuits
  (whole-wheat)

1/2 cup (90g)
  granulated sugar

2 eggs

1 cup (200ml)
  heavy cream

3 tbsp flour

1 tbsp lemon juice

powdered sugar
  --- for topping

[preparation]

Place the cream cheese in a bowl
and bring to room temperature.

Bring the butter to room temperature.

Line the bottom and sides of the pan
with parchment paper.

Preheat the oven to 160-170°C.

1. Put the biscuits into a plastic bag and coarsely crush them with a pestle (or rolling pin), and mix in the butter. Empty the bag in the cake pan. Flip the plastic bag inside out, put your hand inside and press the crumbs evenly and firmly to the bottom of the pan.

2. Beat the cream cheese in the bowl with a hand mixer until soft and smooth.

3. Add granulated sugar and eggs in that order and mix well.

4. Add the heavy cream and mix well till it thickens.

5. Sift in the flour and fold lightly with a rubber spatula. Add the lemon juice and mix some more.

6. Pour the batter into the pan. Holding the edge of the pan, gently lift and drop the pan several times on the counter to let the air out. Bake for 40-45 minutes in a preheated oven.

7. Remove from the oven and set aside to cool. Once it has cooled, remove from the pan and cool in the refrigerator.

   * Baked cheese cake can be kept in the freezer.

8. Slice it into serving-size pieces, and sprinkle powdered sugar to taste.

野 菜 の 切 り 方

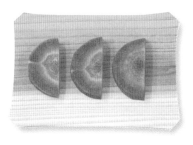

半 月 切 り
Hangetsu-giri
(Half-moons)

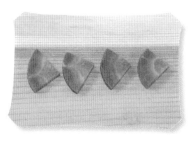

い ち ょ う 切 り
Icho-giri
(Quarter-rounds)

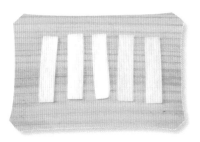

短 冊 切 り
Tanzaku-giri
(Rectangles)

How to cut vegetables

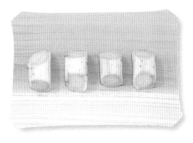

乱 切 り
Ran-giri
(Random-shaped)

く し 形 切 り
Kushigata-giri
(Wedges)

半月切り

半月のように半円形に切る切り方。にんじん、大根、かぶなど筒状の野菜でよく使われる。縦半分にしてから端から料理に合わせた厚さに切る。

Hangetsu-giri (Half-moons)

Cutting ingredients into half-moons. Used for cutting cylindrical vegetables such as carrot, daikon radish, and turnip. Cut vegetables into 2 lengthwise pieces and slice them crosswise to achieve the desired thickness.

いちょう切り

材料の切り方の一つで、いちょうの葉のように扇形に切る切り方。にんじん、大根、かぶなど筒状の野菜でよく使われる。縦に4つ割りにしてから端から薄切りにする。

Icho-giri (Quarter-rounds)

Cutting ingredients into quarter-rounds in the shape of a ginkgo leaf. Used for cutting cylindrical vegetables such as carrot, daikon radish, and turnip. Cut the vegetables into 4 lengthwise pieces and slice them crosswise.

短冊切り

材料を小さな短冊のように、薄く長方形に切る切り方。はじめに求める長さ、幅の直方体に切ってから、端から薄く切る。炒め物や汁の実の野菜や、のりなどを切るときに。

Tanzaku-giri (Rectangles)

Cutting ingredients into thin rectangles. Cut ingredients into pieces of the desired length and width, then slice them into thinner pieces. Suitable for cutting nori or vegetables for stir-fried dishes and soups.

乱切り

材料を不規則な形に切る切り方。材料を回しながら
繊維を断つように切る。大きさは料理によって変わ
るが、均一にすることが大切。切り口の表面積が増
えるので、火の通りが早く、味がしみやすくなる。煮
物や汁物の具などに向いた切り方。

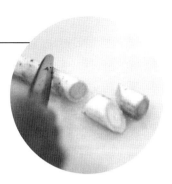

Ran-giri (Random-shaped)

Cutting ingredients into random-shaped but even-sized pieces. Cut the ingredient
diagonally against the grain and rotate it. This ensures a large surface area of the
ingredients, so you can cook these random-shaped wedges rapidly and season
them thoroughly. Suitable for cutting ingredients for simmered dishes and soups.

くし形切り

玉ねぎやトマト、レモンなど、球形の材料を放射状に切る切り方。まず縦半分に切
り、中心から外に向かって均等に切り分ける。

Kushigata-giri (Wedges)

Cutting spherical ingredients such as onion, tomato, and lemon into wedges. Cut
the ingredient into 2 lengthwise pieces and cut them radially into even-sized pieces.

野 菜 の 切 り 方

そ ぎ 切 り

Sogi-giri

(Shaving cut)

さ さ が き

Sasagaki

(*Sasagaki* shavings)

How to cut vegetables

長ねぎの
みじん切り

Fine chopping
(for Japanese leeks)

白髪ねぎ

Shiraga-negi
(White hair leek)

そぎ切り

材料を薄くそぐようにして切る切り方。包丁を斜めにねかせ、手前に引くようにして切る。材料の厚みをそろえたり、表面積を大きくしたいときなどに向いている切り方。

Sogi-giri (Shaving cut)

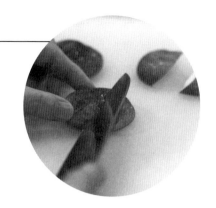

Shaving ingredients thinly. Place a knife flatly against the ingredient and slice it by pulling the knife toward you. Suitable to ensure the even thickness of pieces or to cut pieces with a large surface area.

ささがき

棒状の材料を手に持って回しながら、鉛筆を削るようにして、端から薄くそいでいく切り方。ごぼうを切るときによく用いられる。

Sasagaki (*Sasagaki* shavings)

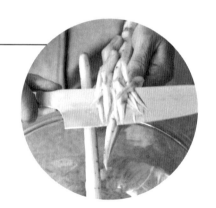

Sasagaki is one way to slice vegetables and is used for shaving long and narrow vegetables like Japanese burdock root. Keep the vegetable in your hand and while you rotate it, shave or slice thinly with a knife as if sharpening a pencil.

長ねぎのみじん切り

長ねぎをみじん切りにするときは、最初に包丁の先でねぎ全体を刺すように細かく切り込みを入れる。その後、端から細かく刻む。さらに細かくしたい場合は、包丁でたたく。

Fine chopping (for Japanese leeks)

Make scores in a Japanese leek with the tip of a knife. Slice it crosswise into small pieces. If necessary, chop these into smaller pieces.

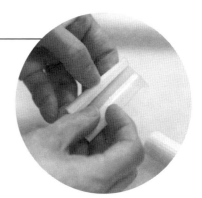

白髪ねぎ

長ねぎの白い部分をごく細いせん切りにしたもの。4 cmくらいの長さに切った後、縦に切り込みを入れて芯を取り、外側の白い部分だけを平らに広げて重ね、繊維に沿って細く切る。その後、水にさらしてから水けをきる。麺類や料理のあしらいなどに。

Shiraga-negi (White hair leek)

Cutting the white part of a Japanese leek into julienne strips. Cut a Japanese leek into 4cm-long pieces. Score the pieces lengthwise, open them, and remove the core. Unfold and pile the remaining layers of the leek and cut along the grain into julienne strips. Soak them in water, drain, and use as a garnish for noodles and other dishes.

スタッフ

撮影：新田みのる、モニカ・ヴァイスマン、デレック・マキシマ
スタイリング：福泉響子
デザイン：粟辻デザイン　粟辻美早、仁科悦子
執筆協力：浅野未華
英語翻訳：小島エリ子
撮影協力：田島 剛（株式会社ペックス）
校正：中沢悦子
編集：湯原一憲（NHK出版）

Harumi

2018（平成30）年5月20日　第1刷発行

著　者　　栗原はるみ
　　　　　©2018　Harumi Kurihara
発行者　　森永公紀
発行所　　NHK出版
　　　　　〒150-8081 東京都渋谷区宇田川町41-1
　　　　　電話　0570-002-042（編集）
　　　　　　　　0570-000-321（注文）
　　　　　ホームページ http://www.nhk-book.co.jp
　　　　　振替　00110-1-49701
印　刷　　共同印刷
製　本　　共同印刷

Printed in Japan
ISBN978-4-14-033299-3　　C2077